What on Earth Are You Doing for Heaven's Sake?

Leonard E. Stadler

Bristol House

WHAT ON EARTH ARE YOU
DOING FOR HEAVEN'S SAKE?
© 2001 by Leonard E. Stadler
Published by Bristol Books, an imprint of Bristol House, Ltd.

First Edition, December 2001

Unless otherwise indicated, all Scripture quotations are from the *New King James Version* © 1979, 1980, 1982 by Thomas Nelson Publishers, Nashville, Tennessee.

All rights reserved. Except for brief quotations embodied in critical articles and reviews, no part of this book may be used or reproduced in any manner whatsoever without written permission.

ISBN: 1-885224-37-0

Printed in the United States of America.

Cover design by Larry Stuart.

Bristol House, Ltd.
P.O. Box 4020
Anderson, Indiana 46013-0020
Phone: 765-644-0856
Fax: 765-622-1045

To order call: 1-800-451-READ (7323)

For my family,
Shana, Shalen and LenPaul,
with much love and appreciation.

Contents

Foreword 5

Introduction 7

1. What Is It Worth to You? 13
2. Keeping the Main Thing
   the Main Thing 21
3. Journey Toward the Son 29
4. The Heavenly Cheerleader 37
5. Jebel Musa 45
6. Chariots of Fire 53
7. The Power to Choose 61
8. When King Uzziah Dies 69
9. The Gospel According to You 75
10. Spiritual Seasons of the Soul ... 81
11. The Laws of Light 89
12. Where Are You? 95
13. It's Just a Matter of Trust 103
14. Kamikaze Christians 111
15. Resurrection Power! 119

Foreword

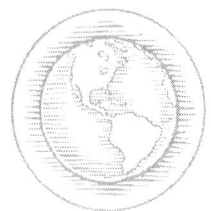

Some writers have the ability to communicate the important truth that life is short and uncertain. We need to evaluate our lives and make the most of every day. Lenny Stadler has that unique ability and communicates it so effectively in *What on Earth Are You Doing for Heaven's Sake?*

I believe that we are living in a period of history when people are taking life and the quality of life much more seriously. Since the events of September 11, 2001, everybody has a different perspective on life. We can never take tomorrow for granted.

The most important thing in life is not how many years we live but how much we live each year. Our lives need to count for something that is of eternal worth. We need to have a fresh, new perspective on our value systems. We cannot control the length of our lives, but we can control the width and depth of our living!

The quality of life hinges on the decisions we make. It is important to notice that the word "life" has a big "if" right in the middle. It hinges on choices. Each choice has a consequence.

Every person has the same number of minutes in each hour and the same number of hours in each day. Each day should be an experience of receiving God's blessings and sharing them with others. We never get to relive a day.

I have been challenged by the following experience written by Ann Walls:

> My brother-in-law opened the bottom drawer of my sister's bureau and lifted out a tissue wrapped package. He said, "This is not a slip, this is lingerie."
>
> He discarded the tissue and handed me the slip. It was exquisite: silk, handmade, and trimmed with a cobweb of lace. The price tag with an astronomical figure on it was still attached.
>
> He said, "Jan bought this the first time we went to New York at least eight or nine years ago. She never wore it. She was saving it for a special occasion. Well, I guess this is the occasion."
>
> He took the slip from me and put it on the bed with the other clothes that we were taking to the mortician. His hands lingered on the soft material for a moment, then he slammed the drawer shut and turned to me and said, "Don't ever save anything for a special occasion. Everyday that you are alive is a special occasion."

Lenny Stadler reminds us that every day is a special occasion and is pregnant with possibilities of how God can use us for things that will last for eternity. He writes in an easy style to understand, but uses that style to confront us with the necessity of choosing our values.

It is a powerful question for the day in which we live—*What on Earth Are You Doing for Heaven's Sake?*

Dr. John Ed Mathison
Frazer Memorial United Methodist Church
Montgomery, Alabama

Introduction

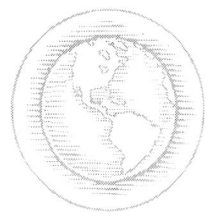

Now you are the body of Christ, and members individually. And God has appointed these in the church: first apostles, second prophets, third teachers, after that miracles, then gifts of healings, helps, administrations, varieties of tongues. Are all apostles? Are all prophets? Are all teachers? Are all workers of miracles? Do all have gifts of healings? Do all speak with tongues? Do all interpret? But earnestly desire the best gifts. And yet I show you a more excellent way (1 Corinthians 12:27–31).

When I was a young boy, I had the reputation of being mischievous. In many ways, I was a real "Little Johnny." I was always saying things with a slight "twist" that should not be said and getting into something that was off-limits. On many occasions, my grandmother (and others) would say to me, "Lenny, what on earth are you doing?" Other times she would say, "For heaven's sake, Lenny, what are you doing?" This question relates to our living the Christian faith on a daily basis.

In 1 Corinthians 12 the Apostle Paul reminds us that in the church there are "varieties of gifts." We do not all have the same spiritual gift, such as apostleship, preaching, teaching or gifts of miracles and healings. Paul says that we should "earnestly desire the higher gifts." If we keep reading, we move into Paul's famous "Love Chapter," 1 Corinthians 13.

What is Paul saying? Not all of us can preach the sermon; not all of us can sing in the choir; not all of us can teach the lesson—but there is one thing we can all do. We can give our love and our best to Christ and to His church! What on earth are you doing for heaven's sake?

In the *Peanuts* comic strip, Lucy is madly in love with Schroeder, the musician. But she cannot get his attention. Schroeder loves his music and his little piano. He sits on the floor playing his piano with great intensity. He ignores Lucy. She tries to get his attention and win his love but to no avail. Schroeder simply ignores her and keeps playing his toy piano. Finally, Lucy says to him, "Schroeder, do you even know what love is?" Abruptly, Schroeder stops playing. He stands to his feet and recites to Lucy the following: "Love. A noun. It means to be fond of, to have a strong affection for or an attachment/devotion to a person or persons." Then he sits back down and resumes playing his piano. Lucy is stunned. Then she says sarcastically, "On paper, he's great!"

That was how Jesus felt about some of the religious leaders of His day. On paper, they looked great. They acted pious. They sounded religious. They spouted high-sounding theological words and phrases. They rushed to the temple constantly and prayed feverishly. But somehow their religion never got translated into the way they lived or treated other people. They were "churchy" but not compassionate. They spoke about love but never got around to

Introduction

being loving. They were so heavenly bound that they were no earthly good.

As Christians, we are first and foremost a "servant" people, not a "privileged" people. There is always the temptation to look good on paper and never get around to translating our creeds into deeds. This kind of religiosity turned Jesus off. That's why Jesus said, "You will know them by their fruits."

We talk a pretty good game, but our real problem is with actions or inactions, with following through on what we say. We talk too much and do too little. We verbalize so well and actualize so poorly. We speak so eloquently and perform so inadequately. Talking a good game is not enough.

A fisherman was out in his boat. He had fished all day and caught nothing. Finally, his patience ran out. He reached under the seat and pulled out a stick of dynamite. He lit the dynamite and threw it into the lake. When it exploded hundreds of fish came to the surface. He took another stick of dynamite and threw it on the other side of the boat. Again, multitudes of fish came to the surface. Just about then, the game warden saw what was happening and went over to arrest the fisherman. When the game warden began to read the man's rights, the fisherman lighted another stick of dynamite and tossed it in the game warden's boat. He said, "Are you gonna fish, or are you gonna talk?"

Talking a good game is not enough! Only when our words and beliefs are translated into actions can Christianity be authenticated. Furthermore, a good start is not enough. "Always finish what you start," was a principle ingrained in me from early childhood. Jesus set the supreme example of this principle when He spoke His last words on the cross, "It is finished."

It was the summer of 1968 and the world had Olympic fever. From nearly every nation world-class athletes had gathered in Mexico City for the Summer Olympics. Thousands of spectators were on hand. Millions watched on their television sets.

One of the most moving moments in Olympic history occurred at these 1968 games. It happened in the running of the marathon. The runners were gathered at the starting line, the gun sounded, and the twenty-six mile race was underway. It wound through the streets of Mexico City and concluded in the Olympic Stadium. The stadium was packed to capacity, and millions were watching on television as the marathoners ran one by one into the tunnel, around the track and crossed the finish line.

After the race they moved to the awards ceremony. The bronze, silver and gold medals were presented to the three top athletes. The gold medal recipient was standing with glistening eyes as they played his national anthem and raised the flag of his country.

Following the awards ceremony, people began to think about other events and turned to watch other athletes who were performing in the stadium. Sometime later, however, a murmur buzzed through the crowd when the people in the stadium realized that the marathon was not over. A runner was still on the course! The other marathoners had finished over an hour ago. Of course, everyone thought the last runner was in. The young man was from the African nation of Tanzania.

He hobbled into the tunnel, limped onto the track and shuffled agonizingly toward the finish line. He was in great pain. He had been injured in a fall early in the race. Now, his knees were bleeding and swollen. His leg muscles were cramping. Dehydration was setting in, but he never gave up. He kept on running. He refused to quit. Finally, he crossed the finish line and fell to the ground. Medical attendants quickly ran over to administer first aid to him.

A television reporter, fascinated by this young man's determination to run and finish the race in spite of the pain, interviewed the runner hours later. "You were injured early. You were hurting badly. It was obvious that you did not have a chance to win the race. Why didn't you just give up?

Introduction

Why didn't you quit the race?" The marathoner said, "My country did not send me five thousand miles to start the marathon. They sent me here to finish it!"

This story illustrates a great Christian principle. Perseverance is crucial. Determination is essential. It is important to finish what we start. It is not enough to make a good beginning. It is not enough to run well part of the way. We must finish what we start and see it through.

Hebrews 12:1 states that we should "lay aside every weight, and the sin which so easily ensnares us, and let us run with endurance the race that is set before us, looking unto Jesus, the author and finisher of our faith, who for the joy that was set before Him endured the cross, despising the shame, and has sat down at the right hand of the throne of God."

Those who have gone before us in the Christian faith have completed their earthly race. They have passed the baton to us and now cheer us on from the heavenly grandstand. Though we are still running the race, we must concentrate on the finish and on Jesus who crossed the finish line and sits at the right hand of God. This brings us to our question: What on earth are you doing for heaven's sake?

Chapter 1

What Is It Worth to You?

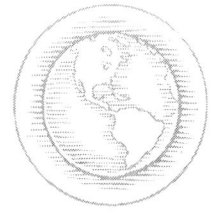

Paul, an apostle of Jesus Christ by the will of God, To the saints who are in Ephesus, and faithful in Christ Jesus:
Grace to you and peace from God our Father and the Lord Jesus Christ.
Blessed be the God and Father of our Lord Jesus Christ, who has blessed us with every spiritual blessing in the heavenly places in Christ, just as He chose us in Him before the foundation of the world, that we should be holy and without blame before Him in love, having predestined us to adoption as sons by Jesus Christ to Himself, according to the good pleasure of His will, to the praise of the glory of His grace, by which He made us accepted in the Beloved.
In Him we have redemption through His blood, the forgiveness of sins, according to the riches of His grace which He made to abound toward us in all

wisdom and prudence, having made known to us the mystery of His will, according to His good pleasure which He purposed in Himself, that in the dispensation of the fullness of the times He might gather together in one all things in Christ, both which are in heaven and which are on earth—in Him. In Him also we have obtained an inheritance, being predestined according to the purpose of Him who works all things according to the counsel of His will, that we who first trusted in Christ should be to the praise of His glory (Ephesians 1:1–12).

· ·

How much are you worth? That is, how much will you spend on consumer goods in a lifetime? A lot of people know the value of things around them—but they often do not know their own value or how much they will spend on consumer products. The Coca-Cola Company has put a $6,000 value on you as a consumer over a lifetime. This means that the next time you buy a Coke, do not think of it as costing a dollar. Think of it as a down payment on that $6,000!

As a lifetime customer General Motors has determined that you are worth about $276,000. Computer companies estimate that the lifetime value of a sophisticated computer user is $45,000. If you are a nontechnical person who puts off computer purchases as long as possible, you have a lifetime value of only $20,000.

Today we read that companies are building their marketing strategies around this lifetime value of a person. Today's marketers focus on the lifetime value of a loyal customer, not just the sales in one quarter.

Yet in stark contrast to this consumer mentality, there are not enough zeroes in a number to indicate the value that God places on you. You are infinitely valuable to God—so much so that He was willing to send His only Son, Jesus

Christ, to die for you so that your sins could be forgiven. No one can put a price tag on that.

God's strategy is not just on a lifetime value. Your worth to God has eternal value—it is numerically unending and cannot be computed. God has promised to walk with you over the mountains and to carry you through the valleys. You are worth more to God than you will ever know! *The question is what is your life worth to you?*

Life Is Worth Living

Some people try to explain life's events by heredity and environment or by coincidence and luck. Then there are people who see a purpose behind this massive universe and that we are all somehow connected. They refer to cosmic forces—as in the Star Wars movies when Luke Skywalker discovers and follows *The Force*. Some people talk about a destiny that we cannot escape. Others talk about how a reason exists for everything that happens to us.

People's reactions to life's events are as different as day and night. Some people become hardened by life. They shake their fists at heaven and ask God why He allows certain things to happen. Others fall to their knees and say, "What will be will be!"

Advertisements for palm readers are a depressing landmark in our culture today. People travel to these seers because they want to know their fate—their destiny—their future.

"I have been diagnosed with an illness; I need to go to a fortune-teller." "I am in a troubled marriage; I need to go to a psychic." "I have spent the last of my investments; I need to seek the advice of a palm reader." Palm readers and psychics pull information out of people and then tell them what they want to hear. Scripture tells us that we are not to seek wisdom from psychics but are to seek and consult our God for direction. Nevertheless, we are curious about the future and sometimes we panic because we know we do not hold the cards.

Following the 2000 presidential election between Governor George W. Bush and Vice President Al Gore, the American people quickly became impatient about the outcome of the election. Regarding that election, I read an ominous statement on the Internet attributed to Joseph Stalin: "It doesn't matter who votes, it matters only who counts the votes."

God is ultimately in control and has a purpose for each of us. The Bible speaks clearly to this point in both Testaments. Each purpose is unique in God's kingdom. Some purposes may be rewarded in this life; many may not. When it is finally revealed, God's purpose for you may even surprise you—as it probably will others.

Have you ever heard the phrase, "sailing under sealed orders"? Anyone who has served in the Navy knows what this means. The hit movie *U-571* demonstrates the meaning. The submarine was in dock at midnight. The crew was ready to sail, but they did not know where they were going or the nature of their mission. The captain held a sealed envelope on which was stamped the words "sailing under sealed orders." Additionally, printed on the outside of the envelope were coordinates of latitude and longitude—a place out on the ocean to which they were to sail.

For the sake of military secrecy, the captain had been trained not to open the envelope until he arrived at that location on the ocean. The ship and crew set sail, not knowing where they were going. They could only trust the captain. When the ship reached the assigned coordinates, the captain revealed the mission.

In one sense, the Christian faith is like that. We do not receive all the information for our lives at once. We move along, placing our confidence in God. We "sail under sealed orders" until we get to a place where God says, "Okay, you've made it this far. Now here is your next move." What is your life worth? The biblical witness is clear: God says your life is worth living.

Chapter 1: What Is It Worth to You?

People Are Worth Loving

They are worth loving not for anything they can do. Every person is a child of God who is created in His image. Sometimes being a member of the human race gets a bad rap. God loves each person so much that He has placed His stamp on you. You are created in His image. You belong to Him. This is why you are worth loving and why people are worth loving!

The movie character Simon Birch was born no bigger than a man's fist. Doctors said he would not live through his first night. He did. Then they said he would not live more than a week, but he did. Weeks turned into months. Then those months turned into years, until Simon grew into a boy. Simon, at age twelve, was so small that he still played the infant Jesus in the church Christmas pageant. Nevertheless, he believed that God had a special plan for his life.

One day Simon Birch approached his pastor on this very question: "Pastor, do you believe God has a plan for our lives?" It was something Simon believed in strongly, but he wanted the pastor to confirm his feelings. Unfortunately, the pastor responded ambiguously, "I don't really know." It was not the answer Simon had hoped for. But even in the face of the pastor's doubt you could see the gleam of faith in the young boy's face. Though Simon Birch lived only twelve years, he believed his life had purpose and that it mattered to God.

Our purpose has nothing to do with age or education or any other measurable external value. Purpose is something you cannot reach in isolation from God's will. Purpose is defined in terms of what God's plan is for us.

Years ago a wealthy English family was entertaining friends in their home. As the children swam in the pond, one ventured into the deep water and began to drown. The gardener's son jumped into the water and saved the child. The child's name was Winston Churchill. Deeply grateful to the young hero, Churchill's parents paid for the boy to study medicine.

Years later when Sir Winston was prime minister of Great Britain, he became very ill with pneumonia. The best physician in Great Britain was called to the bedside of the ailing leader. His name was Sir Alexander Fleming, the developer of penicillin and the boy who long ago had saved Churchill's life. Winston Churchill later said, "Rarely has a man owed his life twice to the same person." People are worth loving—no matter who they are or where they are!

Christ Is Worth Following

Listen to what Paul writes to the church at Ephesus, as J. B. Phillips translates it: ". . . consider what [Christ] has done." God proclaims us citizens of heaven; God chose us even before the foundation of the world; God planned that we should be adopted as His own children through Jesus Christ; through God's only Son, Jesus Christ, and His shed blood we are redeemed and freely forgiven.

Do you think when the prophet Samuel anointed that young boy named David that he suddenly became a king? David might have sensed that one day he would be king, but it took him a lifetime to learn to *be* a king. He never "fully arrived." After David became king he entered upon a constant process of growth.

So it is with the Christian life. God tells us who we are. "You are a Christian, now become like my Son, Jesus Christ." We will never "arrive" at the state of spiritual maturity of Jesus, yet God has claimed us as "sons and daughters."

A Christian author who experienced great tragedy in her family was able to use that pain to minister to other people in pain. Her husband was severely injured in Vietnam. A drunk driver killed her older son. Her husband and she had been alienated from their younger son for years by his choice to experiment with drugs. The Christian author wrote something that struck a chord in my heart. It might make sense to you who are football fans: "God never promised that we would be ahead at halftime. God just promised that we would win the game."

God has a purpose for us. He is not simply sitting in heaven pushing buttons at will as we go along. God does not invade our free will to make us obey Him. What is clear is that we are loved; we are purchased; we are stamped as one of His. We have the guarantee that God will complete His redemption. He knows the rest of the story. Before we waste money on fortune-tellers or read our daily horoscopes, we are to read and trust God's Word. When we do, we will discover that life is worth living, people are worth loving and Jesus is worth following.

What on earth will you do for heaven's sake when you find out what it's worth to you?

Chapter 2

Keeping the Main Thing the Main Thing

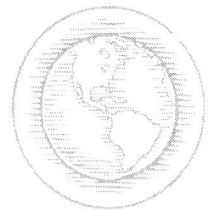

And Jesus came and spoke to them, saying, "All authority has been given to Me in heaven and on earth. Go therefore and make disciples of all the nations, baptizing them in the name of the Father and of the Son and of the Holy Spirit, teaching them to observe all things that I have commanded you; and lo, I am with you always, even to the end of the age" (Matthew 28:18–20).

My former bishop often made a statement that had a great deal of truth in it regardless of the endeavor in which he was involved. We sometimes played golf together, and one day he hit a really bad shot. He looked at me and said, "Now, Lenny, the main thing is to keep the main thing the main thing." I asked, "What do you mean?" He replied, "You gotta keep the ball in the fairway—that's the main thing!"

This is true in any area of life, whether it is business, politics, military or the church. Forgetting this priority has led many people into ruin. Underscore this statement: "Keep the main thing the main thing." It is very easy to let the main thing gradually get pushed back in life, or, as my wife likes to say, "Lenny, don't major in the minors."

The main thing in the life of a Christian and the church is to bring people to Jesus Christ and disciple them in the Christian faith.

The Great Commission is the summation of the main thing: "All authority has been given to Me in heaven and on earth. Go therefore and make disciples of all the nations, baptizing them in the name of the Father and of the Son and of the Holy Spirit, teaching them to observe all things I have commanded you; and lo, I am with you always, even to the end of the age."

These were the marching orders given by Jesus to all who would follow Him and become His disciples. You can hear it in many other statements made by Jesus: "Preach the gospel to every creature . . . I will make you fishers of men . . . You shall be witnesses unto me . . . But you shall receive power when the Holy Spirit has come upon you to be my witnesses in all Jerusalem, Judea, Samaria, and to the end of the earth."

The Great Commission has not changed. You and I are under the same orders. We are soldiers of Christ in the army of God. The Great Commission is the bottom line. It is the main thing as to what Jesus would have you and me do.

Now you would think that something as important as this would grab the attention and conviction of every Christian. Unfortunately, it has not. A majority of Christians in America today have never led anyone to Christ. Yet this is happily changing.

Three reasons stand out regarding our need to fulfill the Great Commission and why this should be our top priority.

Reason Number One: The Messenger

The first reason to keep the Great Commission the main thing is because of God's Messenger—Jesus Christ. He is the King of kings and the Lord of lords. He is the Head of the Church. He is our Commander-in-chief. He has commanded us to go and to make disciples of all nations. On that basis every Christian and every church should be actively engaged in leading and bringing people to Christ.

Off the New England coast lies a dangerous reef that juts into the ocean about a half-mile. It has caused the destruction of many ships. The U.S. Coast Guard has a station there to aid ships that might run aground on the reef.

One night in the middle of a fierce storm, the alarm sounded, and the commander gave the word, "Man the boats!" A ship had run aground on the reef and was breaking up on the waves. A lieutenant said to the commander, "Sir, there is no use. The waves are twelve to fifteen feet high. We cannot possibly go out." The commander snapped, "I have given the order to man the boats." The lieutenant saluted and headed back to the beach. He was a man under orders.

But he came back and said, "Sir, there is just no way. Even if we could possibly get out beyond those breakers, we could never get back again." The commander looked at his officer and said, "Lieutenant, we have to go out! We do not have to come back."

Multitudes of Christians went out and witnessed for Christ and never came back to their homes again! The roster of the martyrs is a very thick book! The word "martyr" comes from the Greek word *martureto,* which literally means "to witness." When so many Christians died for the faith, the word soon came to be known as "to give your life for what you believe and know to be true."

Because they believed, they had to go out—but they did not have to come back! Do we have that same spirit? We are men and women under orders. We must go out!

In 1929 a young man in Kansas named John Griffin had a wife and a baby boy. He had great dreams in life to see the world. But the dust storms that followed the Wall Street crash of 1929 blew all of that away. The winds destroyed not only his crops but also all of his dreams. He packed up their belongings and headed east with his family to look for a job. At the Mississippi River he found work operating a drawbridge for trains.

The years passed and it was 1935. Griffin decided that it was time for his son, Greg, to spend the day with him at work. Little Greg was only six years old. He watched as his father went into the great control room and pushed the levers to roll the bridge up into the sky. Trains then roared across the bridge. Little Greg was greatly impressed that his father was in charge of such an operation.

At noontime, Griffin put the bridge up, knowing that a train would not be coming for some time. He and his son walked out over a catwalk to a little platform. As they ate their lunch, he told his son about the destinations of the ships and trains.

The time quickly slipped by and he suddenly heard the train whistle. He looked at his watch and realized that it was the #107—the Memphis Express. It would come roaring out of the woods to cross the river. Realizing that he had time, he did not panic. He said to his son, "You stay right where you are." He walked back along the catwalk and climbed up the ladder into the control room. He looked up and down the river to see if any boats were coming. Suddenly, he saw a sight that caused his heart to leap right into his throat. His little boy had attempted to follow him back and had fallen off the catwalk into a massive gear room. The boy was still conscious but his left leg was trapped in the main gear. The train was quickly approaching the bridge. Griffin had to make a decision. Four hundred people were on that train. But this was his only son. He knew what he had to do, so he buried his head in his arms and pushed the

Chapter 2: Keeping the Main Thing the Main Thing   25

lever. The bridge came down just in time for the train to cross the river. He lifted his tear-stained face. Being unable to look below, he looked into the passing windows of the train. He saw businessmen reading the daily paper, the conductor looking at his watch, and ladies sipping tea in the dining car. But no one looked at him. He pounded on the window and yelled, "What's wrong with you people, don't you care? Don't you realize I gave my son for you?"

In the book of Lamentations the prophet said, "Is it nothing to you, all you who pass by? Behold and see if there is any sorrow like my sorrow, which has been brought on me" (1:12).

The bridge had to be lowered into place. Jesus is that bridge between heaven and earth.

I was in Jerusalem showing a group of people the face of a hillside known as Gordon's Calvary. Many believe this is the place where the crucifixion took place. On the face of the hill you can see the outlines of eyes, a nose, and a mouth—forming the semblance of a skull. That is why it is called Golgotha, "the place of the skull." But right at the base of the hill is a bus station. Buses pass right by the hill. So many people passing by Calvary without noticing what God has done for them. How can we not fulfill the Great Commission after what Christ has done for us?

Reason Number Two: The Message

The second reason to keep the Great Commission the main thing is because of the message to the world that we must proclaim. Millions around the world do not have the faintest idea what the gospel really means. There is such a shallow understanding of the Good News in today's world. We need to take the message to the lost because they have no other hope. God is counting on you and me.

An apocryphal story about the time Jesus returned from earth to heaven has all the angels and archangels listening as Jesus tells them about His birth in a stable, His life as a carpenter and His ministry to the sick. He tells them of His cross at Jerusalem, His resurrection, and ascension into heaven. He describes His telling the disciples that they were to take God's message of salvation into the entire world. One of the angels asked, "But, Lord, what if they don't do it? What other plan have you?" Jesus says, "I have no other plan."

There is no other plan apart from us. It is our job to go and tell others that they have no other Savior than Jesus Christ.

The world is full of religions and religious teachers, but there is only one Savior. The only thing that keeps us out of God's kingdom is our sin. And only Jesus died for our sin. The great religions of the world teach salvation by human merit. Only Christianity teaches salvation by grace. There are many religions but there's only one gospel. All other religions say, "do," but Christ says, "done." It is finished!

Reason Number Three: The Mission

The third reason we should keep the Great Commission the main thing is simply because it is the mission of every Christian. In fact it is implied in the very name, *Christian*. It is who we are and what we are to do as Christians!

Alexander the Great had conquered the whole world by the time he was thirty-three years old. He wept because there were no more worlds to conquer. One of the most outstanding qualities about Alexander was that he was fearless. The one thing he despised was cowardice. In fact, Alexander would ride out in front of his army. None of the Persian spears and arrows brought him down.

After conquering the world, he made Babylon his headquarters. One day he was holding court for his army in a vast hall that was built by Nebuchadnezzar. Soldiers lined the wall with spears by their sides. Alexander sat on his throne.

Chapter 2: Keeping the Main Thing the Main Thing

The master of arms brought out a group of soldiers. Charges against them were read aloud in the great hall. No lawyers were present to plead their cases. Alexander pronounced their sentences on the spot. No court of appeals was available for them. Alexander passed the death sentence on many that day.

Then they brought out a young man, probably no older than 18 years of age, a striking Macedonian with blond hair and blue eyes. Alexander looked at him as one read the charge. He had fled in the face of the enemy and had been found cringing in a cave. Alexander said to him, "Son, what is your name?" Everyone in the room breathed a sigh of relief. They knew he had won the king's heart. The boy also sighed and said, "Alexander."

Suddenly, the smile left the king's face and he said, "What is your name?" The boy snapped to attention and said, "Alexander, sir!" The king loudly said, "What is your name?" The boy began to stammer, "Alexander, sir." The king exploded out of his chair and grabbed the boy by his tunic. Throwing him to the ground he said, "Soldier, change your conduct or change your name!"

More often than not, Christians are like that young soldier. We, too, have turned and fled in the face of the Adversary. We have been concerned when threatened, not with spears and arrows, but with a raised eyebrow, a smirk, a laugh, a word of rejection. It is all that has been needed to silence us. But God wants to infuse us with the Spirit of Jesus Christ so that we might have His courage and endeavor to keep the Great Commission the main thing!

What on earth will you do for heaven's sake when you keep the main thing the main thing?

Chapter 3

Journey Toward the Son

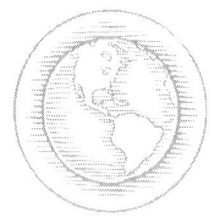

By faith Abraham obeyed when he was called to go out to the place which he would receive as an inheritance. And he went out, not knowing where he was going. By faith he dwelt in the land of promise as in a foreign country, dwelling in tents with Isaac and Jacob, the heirs with him of the same promise; for he waited for the city which has foundations, whose builder and maker is God (Hebrews 11:8–10).

The metaphor of *journey* is important in our understanding of the dynamic of Christian faith. Abraham dramatically symbolizes the Christian life as a journey. Abraham lived in Ur of the Chaldees, which is modern-day Iraq. The Chaldeans were moon worshipers. Before he received the call of God, Abraham was probably a moon worshiper. God spoke to Abraham and said, "Leave this country and go to a place I will show you." So Abraham left his home—the familiar and comfortable place where he had complete control and security.

He then began his journey of faith toward the unknown. Abraham had no idea where he was going. When he reached the land of promise, he continued to live there as a stranger in a strange land. Abraham looked for the city whose foundation and architect was God.

Like Abraham, we too are on a journey. Ur of the Chaldees is analogous to our pre-Christian life. God breaks into our lives and into our world in the person of Jesus Christ and says, "Follow Me." We begin our journey of faith when we leave the security and the things that we think we can control, which we give over to Jesus. We follow Christ by faith into the unknown future. Ultimately, it is a journey toward the Son of God Himself.

I heard of a man who was on a different kind of journey. He walked *backward* across the United States. He started in California and ended in New York. When he finished this incredible feat someone asked him, "What was the single, most difficult part of your trip? Was it the desert, the rivers, the mountains or the traffic?" "None of these," answered the man, "It was the sand in my shoes!"

This story has an obvious meaning for us in the busy, hectic world in which we live. Our journey of faith is not threatened by the big obstacles we face but by a multitude of little strains and stresses that build up over time.

As a matter of fact, most of us manage the major emergencies of life well enough. The great trials of sorrow, tragedy and hardship are often handled with poise and strength and sometimes even with heroism. When crises come, most of us tend to rise to the occasion. It is those little stresses and strains in life that tend to wear us down.

As we journey toward the Son, it is often the sand in our shoes that cripples and depletes our souls. The little things in life and the way we handle or mishandle them can make a big difference in where we come out.

What destroys marriages? More often than not it is the little things that erode the endearing relationship between husband and wife. What alienates families? Often it is the little things that build up over time. What cripples the church more than any other thing? Usually, it is the sand in our shoes.

What about the sand in your shoes today? What are those little things that so easily distract and upset you? Is sand in your shoes hindering you in your journey of faith or keeping you from being all that God wants you to be?

Internal Worries

Little internal worries are like sand in our shoes. Those little worries and nagging anxieties can destroy us. We can handle the big problems fairly well. But those little worries can easily become the sand in our shoes. Someone once prayed, "Lord, we can handle the elephants but please deliver us from these gnats."

On the slope of Long's Peak in Colorado lie the ruins of a gigantic tree. This tree once stood for 400 years. It was a seedling when Columbus arrived in San Salvador. It was a fourth grown when the pilgrims settled in Plymouth. During the course of 400 years, that tree was struck by lightning at least fourteen times. Countless avalanches descended upon it and storms pounded it—but the tree stood. However, in the end the great tree fell to the ground. An army of tiny beetles attacked the tree and eventually brought it down. The little insects ate their way through the bark and gradually destroyed the inner strength of the tree by their persistent attacks.

This great forest tree that age could not wither, lightning could not destroy, avalanches could not push over, storms could not shatter, fell at last because tiny beetles attacked it.

Little worries are like those tiny insects. They may be small but they incessantly eat away at our inner strength.

Little worries attack and burrow their way inward, devastating our inner strength until we become so weak that it results in a fall.

External Pressure Points

Second, little external pressure points are like sand in our shoes. It usually happens in our daily routines. Even casual acquaintances or friends can apply pressure points on us without realizing it.

A man of Italian ancestry had always dreamed of visiting Italy and meeting the pope. He saved his money and finally had enough to make the trip. Just before he was about to leave he went for a haircut. The barber asked, "What airline are you using to go to Italy?"

"I'm flying Alitalia Airlines."

The barber said, "Forget it. They've got a terrible reputation; you'll be sorry. Where are you going to stay?"

The man said, "I'll be staying at the Hilton in Rome."

The barber groaned, "Forget it. They've got terrible service. What are you going to do when you're in Rome?"

The man said, "I'm going to see the pope."

The barber laughed, "Forget it. You'll never see the pope. You're a nobody. The pope sees only important people. You're wasting your time and money!"

Several weeks later the same man returned to the barbershop. The barber said, "So, I bet you never got to Italy." The man replied, "As a matter of fact, I did. I flew Alitalia and they were just wonderful to me. When I got to Rome I stayed at the Hilton and they treated me like a king."

"What did you do when you got there?" the barber asked.

"I went to see the pope."

"Well," the barber said impatiently, "What happened?"

The man said, "I knelt and kissed the pope's ring."

"Wow!" the barber said, "You kissed the pope's ring! What did he say?"

"Well, the pope looked down at me and said, 'My son, where did you get that terrible haircut?'"

Dr. Richard Hoffman of New York says that the three major killers of our society are not heart disease, cancer and strokes. They are calendars, telephones and clocks! How many of us live under the tyranny of an accelerated life? How many of us allow little external pressure points to become sand in our shoes?

Resentments, Envy and Jealousy

Finally, little resentments, envy and jealousy are like sand in our shoes. They can hinder our journey toward the Son. Do you know what the three miles of love are? The first mile of love is to love the lovable. It is easy to love those who love you back. The second mile of love is to love the unlovable—those who do not love you back. The third mile of love is to love those who succeed where we fail . . . to love those who are more fortunate than we are . . . to love those who landed the job that we wanted.

Once a holy man lived as a hermit in the desert. A group of demons tormented the holy man. They tried to break his spirit by tempting him with wine, women and worldly pleasures—but to no avail. They could not upset him in any way. No matter what they did, he resisted every temptation with peace, confidence and serenity. The holy man was steadfast and immovable. When the devil came along, he saw what was happening. He said to his demons, "You're going about this all wrong. Your methods are too obvious." The devil whispered these words into the ears of the holy man: "Have you heard the news? Your brother has just been made bishop of Alexandria." Immediately, a malignant scowl of jealousy clouded the once serene face of the holy man.

Little worries, little stresses and little resentments—these are the things that so easily can become the sand in our shoes—hindering our journey toward the Son.

How do we get the sand out of our shoes? Let me give you three rapid-fire suggestions: First, on your journey toward the Son—travel light. Decide what is really important and give your energies to that. Major in the majors and not in the minors.

Second, take only one step at a time. You can live only one day at a time. That is why Jesus said, "Don't be anxious about tomorrow." Finally, trust your whole life into God's care and provision. If you give your life totally and unreservedly to God, then God becomes responsible for the consequences of your life.

In 1973 in the midst of Vietnam and Watergate, a twenty-two-year-old man by the name of Peter Jenkins became so disillusioned with this country that he made plans to move to another country. Then a friend challenged Jenkins to take one more good look at America before making a final decision.

Jenkins accepted the challenge and embarked upon a journey throughout this country accompanied only by his backpack and his faithful dog, Cooper. His travels began in New York and moved southward along the Appalachian Mountains. On the way he met many people and faced many hardships. He feared for his life when accused of being a "drug-dealing hippie." An African-American family in the mountains of North Carolina gave him refuge and friendship. He worked briefly at a religious commune in Tennessee where he grieved over the death of his dog, Cooper.

After two years of walking he made it to New Orleans, and there he decided to attend an old-fashioned tent revival meeting. As he heard the message of the gospel, he gave his life to Jesus Christ. In Louisiana Jenkins also met his future wife.

The details of this life-changing journey have been made known to us through Jenkins's book, *A Walk Across America*. His journey did not stop in New Orleans. He continued by

Chapter 3: Journey Toward the Son

heading west—ultimately to the Pacific Ocean. One day he would even walk across China. But on these other journeys Jenkins would not be alone. Walking with him would be his wife . . . and Jesus Christ. So it is with us on our journey toward the Son. God is with us all the way.

I have often thought about Moses when he encountered God in the burning bush in the Sinai desert. God told him, "Moses, take your shoes off. You're standing on holy ground." Out of fear and reverence Moses obeyed God. Moses had to get the sand out of his shoes before God could use him. And so it is with us.

What on earth will you do for heaven's sake as you journey toward the Son?

Chapter 4

The Heavenly Cheerleader

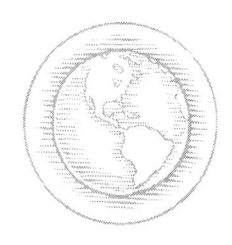

So [Jesus] got into a boat, crossed over, and came to His own city. Then behold, they brought to Him a paralytic lying on a bed. When Jesus saw their faith, He said to the paralytic, "Son, be of good cheer; your sins are forgiven you" (Matthew 9:1–2).

Now in the fourth watch of the night Jesus went to them, walking on the sea. And when the disciples saw Him walking on the sea, they were troubled, saying, "It is a ghost!" And they cried out for fear.
But immediately Jesus spoke to them, saying, "Be of good cheer! It is I; do not be afraid"
(Matthew 14:25–27).

These things I have spoken to you, that in Me you may have peace. In the world you will have tribulation; but be of good cheer, I have overcome the world" (John 16:33).

I enjoy all kinds of sporting events. I enjoy being a spectator, and whenever possible, a participant in sports. One of the things that makes sporting events so exciting is not only the quality of talent and dedication that the athletes display, but those guys and girls who help get the crowd stimulated and charged up about the game. Of course, I am talking about the cheerleaders. When a team becomes discouraged and falls behind in the score, or intimidated by its opponents, the cheerleaders often become factors in the game. Their objective is to get the crowd "turned on." And if the crowd gets into the game, they will "turn on" the team. Many games are won because of confident cheerleaders.

When God called me into the ministry, it was a "tough call." Initially, I ran from the call. But the further I ran, the more discouraged and disheartened I became. In one sense I was lagging behind. I felt intimidated by those who had gone into seminary straight out of college. Then someone said to me, "Lenny, we are in this world for Jesus Christ and God is calling you to be on his team. Don't worry about anything! Jesus Christ is our heavenly Cheerleader."

What a concept! Now this is an earthly image—but it does point to a spiritual reality. In one sense, Jesus Christ is our heavenly Cheerleader. He gives us encouragement when we are discouraged and confidence when we are intimidated by circumstances. He brings comfort when we find ourselves in the midst of sorrow and motivates us when we are lagging behind in our Christian walk. I want to think with you about the three great cheers of the heavenly Cheerleader!

His Pardon

The cheer of His pardon is found in Matthew 9:2 when Jesus said, "Be of good cheer; your sins are forgiven you." Jesus had been on the eastern shore of the Sea of Galilee. This place was known as the land of the Gadarenes. He

Chapter 4: The Heavenly Cheerleader

decided to cross over to Capernaum, headquarters for His Galilean ministry. When He arrived at Capernaum, there was a man who was incapacitated by palsy. This man had been brought to Jesus by four of his friends. Because of the crowd, they lowered this man down through the roof. Jesus saw that he was also crippled by sin.

Is that not true of us in the twentieth century? All of us desire to be in good health. We know we can do more for Christ and His church with healthy bodies, for the body is the temple of the Holy Spirit. But there is something far more incapacitating than physical illness. That spiritually crippling disease is called *sin*.

How many times have we left a worship service inspired and motivated to witness for Christ, but we could not because we were crippled by sin. How many times have we had the good intentions of doing something in the Sunday school, youth group, choir or in a committee, but we found ourselves crippled by sin. How many times has a church really wanted to go forward for Christ and do great things in the community and world, but the church was hampered by conflict. Palsy may be physically incapacitating, but just as spiritually debilitating is the disease called *sin*.

When Jesus looked upon this paralytic man, He gave us our first cheer: "My son, my daughter, be of good cheer; your sins are forgiven you."

Corrie Ten Boom was the Dutch Christian who wrote her famous autobiography, *The Hiding Place*. During one of her speaking engagements in Munich, she testified to God's delivering her out of a Nazi concentration camp. As she looked into the audience, she saw the former SS guard who had stood guard at the shower-room door as the prisoners were marched to their deaths. Can you imagine how she felt as she shared her Christian faith with the former Nazi soldier who had been responsible for killing her sister, Betsy?

When the service was over, the man approached Corrie to shake her hand. At first Corrie tried to smile but could not and her hand was paralyzed by her side. Corrie prayed a silent prayer, "Jesus, I cannot forgive him. Give me your forgiveness." It was in that moment that Corrie heard the heavenly Cheerleader: "Be of good cheer, Corrie, your sins are forgiven you." She took his hand into hers and felt God's love for this stranger. Jesus Christ had given her His forgiveness to forgive him and His love to love even those who are our enemies. The heavenly Cheerleader had set Corrie Ten Boom free.

Have you ever been crippled by sin? Have you ever been bound by unforgiveness? Have you ever prayed and the ceiling above seemed like steel and your prayers just didn't appear to get through? Have you ever wanted to go deeper in your Christian walk, but you felt paralyzed? I have felt that way. But I have good news for you. The heavenly Cheerleader says, "Be of good cheer; your sins are forgiven you." There is a cheerleader in heaven who is cheering for us even now. How I love the cheer of His pardon!

His Presence

The cheer of His presence is found in Matthew 14:27. Jesus said, "Be of good cheer! It is I; do not be afraid."

When Jesus heard about the tragic death of John the Baptist, He was deeply troubled. He withdrew to be alone. Jesus went across to the other side of the Sea of Galilee. Still, the crowd followed Him, and He had great compassion for them. He healed the sick, and that evening He took five loaves and two fish and fed them. While Jesus dismissed the crowds, His disciples got into the boat to cross over to the other side. The sea quickly began to churn as a storm came up. It was during the fourth watch of the night (3 to 6 a.m.) that they saw something coming from Capernaum. They had never seen anything like this before. It appeared that a man was walking on the water! The Bible says they were terribly afraid: "It's a ghost!" But in the middle of their

Chapter 4: The Heavenly Cheerleader

fear and distress, Jesus said: "Be of good cheer! It is I; do not be afraid."

At times we need a touch from Jesus. Nothing else or no one else will do except Jesus. Have you ever had people come to you during the middle of your distress or anxiety and hug you and say, "I understand"? They tried to understand, but they really didn't understand. They had never been there. They had never walked in your shoes. They could not possibly know how much you hurt. They did the best they could, but what you really needed was the assurance of God's presence.

Babe Ruth had hit 714 home runs during his baseball career and was playing one of his last major league games. It was the Braves versus the Reds in Cincinnati. But the great Ruth was no longer so agile as he had once been. He fumbled the ball and threw badly. In one inning alone his errors were responsible for most of the five runs scored by Cincinnati. Babe was no longer hearing the cheers of the crowd.

As the Babe walked off the field after the third out and headed toward the dugout, a crescendo of yelling and booing reached his ears. Just then a boy jumped over the railing onto the playing field. With tears streaming down his face, he threw his arms around the legs of his hero. Ruth did not hesitate for one moment. He picked up the boy and hugged him. He set him down on his feet and patted his head gently. The noise from the stands came to an abrupt halt. Suddenly there was no more booing. In fact, a hush fell over the entire ball park. In those brief moments, the fans saw two heroes: Babe Ruth, who in spite of his poor performance on the field could still care about a little boy; and the small lad, who cared about the feelings of another human being. Both had melted the hearts of the crowd.

Whether in the midst of depression, despair, sorrow, tragedy or loneliness, when the heavenly Cheerleader comes and says, "Be of good cheer! It is I; do not be afraid," we can tackle the world. No problem is too great or circumstance too difficult. When the heavenly Cheerleader gives us the assurance of His presence, we can be more than conquerors.

His Power

The cheer of His power is found in John 16:33 when Jesus said, "In the world you will have tribulation; but be of good cheer, I have overcome the world." One of my favorite places is Jerusalem. If you have never been there, I hope someday you will go on a pilgrimage to the Holy City. The most striking feature of Jerusalem is the medieval wall encircling the Old City. It is two and a half miles in circumference and is thirty-eight feet high on average. The Ottoman Turks, as it appears today, built the wall in the sixteenth century on the foundation that dates back to the time of Christ. Eight gates, seven open and one closed, pierce the wall. On the eastern wall, there are two gates—the Golden Gate and St. Stephen's Gate. Every time I go to Jerusalem, I always enjoy going to St. Stephen's Gate.

Stephen was one of the first seven deacons in the early church. Stephen's life and ministry had challenged the religious status quo of Jerusalem. Stephen confronted his own people, the Jews, and challenged them with the gospel of Jesus Christ. The religious establishment was so infuriated that they took him to the edge of the city and stoned him to death. A man named Saul held their cloaks while they hurled the stones. But Stephen looked into heaven and saw the glory of God and Jesus Christ seated on the right hand of God. In the middle of the terror of being stoned, Stephen needed something that goes beyond human strength. He needed Holy Spirit power. He needed a strength and empowerment that comes only from God. And in the middle of having the life beaten out of his body, Stephen said, "Lord, do not charge them with this sin." No doubt, this made a great impression on the mind of Saul, and shortly thereafter he received salvation in the middle of the road to Damascus. Saul, later called Paul, became the greatest missionary the church has ever known.

Have you ever prayed for people who despised you? Have you prayed for people who talk behind your back? Have you ever been exhausted in human strength and needed God's power?

The only way to live in victory is to receive a power that you and I do not have within ourselves and that is available only through the Holy Spirit. To walk victoriously and to live abundantly we need to hear and receive the cheer of His power. Jesus said, "In the world you will have tribulation; but be of good cheer, I have overcome the world." When the world sees us empowered by the fullness of God's Spirit, then the world is going to say, "Whatever it is you have, I want."

I love the cheer of His pardon. I need the cheer of His presence. But I must have the cheer of His power. With those three cheers, we can become the sons and daughters of God. What a heavenly Cheerleader!

What on earth will you do for heaven's sake when you hear the three great cheers of the heavenly Cheerleader?

Chapter 5

Jebel Musa

Now Moses was tending the flock of Jethro his father-in-law, the priest of Midian. And he led the flock to the back of the desert, and came to Horeb, the mountain of God. And the Angel of the Lord appeared to him in a flame of fire from the midst of a bush. So he looked, and behold, the bush was burning with fire, but the bush was not consumed. Then Moses said, "I will now turn aside and see this great sight, why the bush does not burn."
So when the Lord saw that he turned aside to look, God called to him from the midst of the bush and said, "Moses, Moses!"
And he said, "Here I am."
Then He said, "Do not draw near this place. Take your sandals off your feet, for the place where you stand is holy ground." Moreover He said, "I am the God of your father—the God of Abraham, the God

of Isaac, and the God of Jacob." And Moses hid his face, for he was afraid to look upon God.
And the Lord said: "I have surely seen the oppression of My people who are in Egypt, and have heard their cry because of their taskmasters, for I know their sorrows. So I have come down to deliver them out of the hand of the Egyptians, and to bring them up from that land to a good and large land, to a land flowing with milk and honey, to the place of the Canaanites and the Hittites and the Amorites and the Perizzites and the Hivites and the Jebusites. Now therefore, behold, the cry of the children of Israel has come to Me, and I have also seen the oppression with which the Egyptians oppress them. Come now, therefore, and I will send you to Pharaoh that you may bring My people, the children of Israel, out of Egypt" (Exodus 3:1–10).

....

There is a need for renewed excellence in our land—whether it is in business, education, industry, the church or physical exercise. Bud Wilkinson, the former football coach for the University of Oklahoma, was once asked by a reporter what contribution football had made to physical fitness. His reply was simply: "Absolutely nothing! I define football as twenty-two men on the field who desperately need rest and fifty thousand people in the grandstand who desperately need exercise!"

For Christians, mediocrity should never be acceptable. We should have a desire to surpass the norm, to exceed the commonplace and to excel in all things.

Unfortunately, this is not happening in the church today. For the most part we have allowed the quest for excellence to be replaced by indifference, dissension and disappointment. We substitute convenience for commitment. We allow experiences in the wilderness to sidetrack us from the pursuit of excellence.

Chapter 5: Jebel Musa

Over three thousand years ago, Moses and the children of Israel left Egypt for the freedom of the Promised Land. In one sense, they were in quest of excellence. However, before they could ever reach the Promised Land, they first had to journey through the Sinai.

Few places on earth are as remote and desolate as the "great and terrible wilderness" of the Sinai. In the wilderness the children of Israel encountered conflicts that still beset us today: fear, uncertainty, grief, anger, doubt, discouragement and temptation. These are the constant companions of all of us who are on a spiritual journey from the bondage of sin to spiritual freedom and maturity in Jesus Christ.

There is a tendency, when we come to the end of our own resources, to accuse others of and sometimes to blame God for our problems. In our grief, confusion, faltering faith, adversity or even sin, we may wander as though we are spiritually lost. But like the children of Israel we may discover that such a wilderness journey is actually the point of our true beginning with God.

Yet if we wander long enough, we begin to realize that God allows us to remain in the wilderness in order to *purge* us of our yesterdays and to *prepare* us for the wonderful things in store for tomorrow. It is the quest for excellence.

The Sinai desert remains today as it was in the time of Moses—a giant, scorching crucible that has melted armies, destroyed kings and burned from the hearts of humans both sin and selfishness until they have emerged pure and prepared for God's ministry. Such was the life of Moses.

After living in Egypt for forty years, Moses spent the next forty years in the wilderness. Out of the burning desert, the crucible of the Sinai, Moses emerged not a prince of Egypt but a prophet of God. He returned to Egypt to lead God's people into a land unknown to them but promised by God. The Lord reinforced Moses with signs and miracles. Pharaoh was awed by the determination of the man who had fled from him so many years before. Pharaoh finally succumbed to the pressures of God. The children of Israel were set free to find their way through the Sinai to the land of promise.

The Lord opened the Red Sea to allow the Israelites to pass through, brought water from the desert, delivered manna every morning and gave a great military victory to the Israelites at Rephidim.

At Rephidim a desert people called the Amalekites attacked the Israelites. Moses, with his brother Aaron and another Israelite named Hur, climbed Mount Tahumeh overlooking the battle. As long as Moses stretched out his hands and his wooden staff over the valley below, the Israelite troops, under Joshua, advanced. When his arms grew tired and fell to his side, the Amalekites began winning. To assure victory, Aaron and Hur held up the arms of Moses.

After this victory Moses brought the children of Israel to the base of Mount Sinai. It was here that God had spoken to Moses through the burning bush, and now, God would give the Ten Commandments to His people through Moses.

There, soaring into the rich blue sky at a height of 7,497 feet, are the magnificent three columns of granite at the apex of Mount Sinai. The Bedouin Arabs call it "Jebel Musa," or the "Mountain of Moses."

It is impossible to approach Mount Sinai, much less climb to the summit, without being overwhelmed by the beauty and majesty of the huge mass of granite rock. In the sunset it glows a deep purple; in the light of dawn it flashes red and gold. Without question, this mountain still bears the indelible fingerprint of God.

Three dynamics emerge from Moses' life in the Sinai. They are characteristic of a life spent in pursuit of excellence.

A Call to Action

First, the quest for excellence means there will be a call to action. At the age of eighty, Moses did not give up. He did not yield to a passive, complacent lifestyle. There was no retirement for Moses. He was in the most barren, desolate place on the planet. In order to stay alive, he stayed active.

A certain school custodian was known to exaggerate. A student once asked how old he was. The custodian replied, "Well, I'm forty-seven." The student kept inquiring, "How long have you worked here?" The custodian answered, "Fifty-five years." The puzzled student asked, "But how could you do that?" The custodian grinned and said, "Overtime!"

At the age of eighty Moses heard the voice of God while tending Jethro's flocks near the base of Mount Sinai. It was the first time in 400 years that the Lord had spoken to one of His chosen people. At Mount Sinai, God commissioned Moses: "I am sending you to Pharaoh to bring my people the Israelites out of Egypt" (Exodus 3:10). God's call on the life of Moses was a call to action.

A Call to Adventure

Second, the quest for excellence means there will be a call to adventure. In 1966, while he was unemployed and drifting, Lou Holtz listed on paper 107 lifetime goals. Becoming head coach of the Notre Dame Fighting Irish fulfilled one of those goals. Winning a national championship fulfilled another. Other goals on the list included dinner at the White House, a guest appearance on "The Tonight Show," and ownership of a 1949 Chevrolet. Most of his goals have been realized by now. Lou Holtz's advice is simply this: "Don't be a spectator; don't let life pass you by." Never lose your sense of adventure.

Many people do not want a sense of adventure because it involves too much risk. There is a story about a monastery in Europe that is perched high on a cliff several hundred feet in the air. The only way to reach the monastery is to be suspended in a basket, which is then pulled to the top by several monks. Obviously, there is great risk in riding up the steep cliff in a frail basket. One visitor became exceedingly nervous about halfway up as he noticed that the rope by which the basket was suspended was old and frayed. With a trembling voice he asked the monk who was riding with him how often they changed the rope. The monk thought for a moment and replied, "Whenever it breaks."

It was 3:00 in the morning Jerusalem time when the bus pulled away from the hotel on the Mount of Olives, which overlooks the Holy City. We were headed toward the Sinai Peninsula.

As we made our seven-hour journey, I had difficulty catching much sleep. The very name, "Sinai," stirred my sense of adventure. I recalled many childhood memories of stories about that awesome and holy place. To climb Mount Sinai was one of my great dreams in life. The Egyptian guide said, "You're crazy! It's too hot! Not enough time!"

Nevertheless, five of us started the climb and we finally made it to the summit two hours later. It was an experience that brought the Old Testament to life for me. I was standing on holy ground where Moses had received the Ten Commandments. We read the related Scripture and then made our way back down the mountain. The memories from that experience will be with me for the rest of my life.

A Call to an Expectant Attitude

Third, the quest for excellence means there will be a call to an expectant attitude. The quest for excellence means you can expect great things from a great God.

A farmer who was continually optimistic was seldom discouraged or blue. He had a neighbor who was just the opposite. One day the optimist decided to put his pessimistic neighbor to the test. He bought the smartest, most expensive bird dog he could find. He trained him to do

Chapter 5: Jebel Musa

things no other dog on earth could do—impossible feats that would astound anyone. He invited the pessimist to go duck hunting with him. They sat in the boat hidden behind a duck blind. The ducks flew in. Both men fired and several ducks fell to the water. "Go get 'em!" ordered the optimist with a gleam in his eye. The dog leaped out of the boat, walked on the water and picked up the birds one by one! "Well, what do you think of that?" asked the optimist. Without smiling the pessimist answered, "He can't swim, can he?"

The quest for excellence involves action. God has a call on your life that requires your active participation. The quest for excellence involves adventure. Never lose your sense of adventure. The quest for excellence involves an expectant attitude. "I know the plans I have for you, says the Lord, plans for welfare and not for evil, to give you a future and a hope" (Jeremiah 29:11).

What on earth will you do for heaven's sake when you strive for excellence as Moses did at Jebel Musa?

Chapter 6

Chariots of Fire

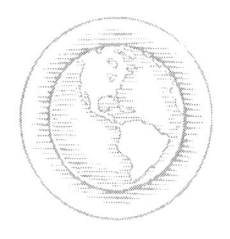

Now the king of Syria was making war against Israel; and he consulted with his servants, saying, "My camp will be in such and such a place." And the man of God sent to the king of Israel, saying, "Beware that you do not pass this place, for the Syrians are coming down there." Then the king of Israel sent someone to the place of which the man of God had told him. Thus he warned him, and he was watchful there, not just once or twice.

Therefore the heart of the king of Syria was greatly troubled by this thing; and he called his servants and said to them, "Will you not show me which of us is for the king of Israel?"

And one of his servants said, "None, my lord, O king; but Elisha, the prophet who is in Israel, tells the king of Israel the words that you speak in your bedroom."

*So he said, "Go and see where he is, that I may send and get him."
And it was told him, saying, "Surely he is in Dothan." Therefore he sent horses and chariots and a great army there, and they came by night and surrounded the city. And when the servant of the man of God arose early and went out, there was an army, surrounding the city with horse and chariots. And his servant said to him, "Alas, my master! What shall we do?"
So he answered, "Do not fear, for those who are with us are more than those who are with them." And Elisha prayed, and said, "Lord, I pray, open his eyes that he may see." Then the Lord opened the eyes of the young man, and he saw. And behold, the mountain was full of horses and chariots of fire all around Elisha (2 Kings 6:8–17).*

....

Billy Sunday was a great evangelist in a former generation. Before Billy Sunday was an evangelist, he played professional baseball for the Chicago White Sox. One day he was playing in left field. A long fly ball was hit in his direction. He ran as fast as he could and reached as high as he could. Wondrously, he caught that ball! When the game was over, a news reporter came up to him and congratulated him on making an outstanding catch. Billy Sunday replied, "Well, it really wasn't a fair catch because I prayed."

The reporter inquired, "You prayed. What did you say in your prayer?"

"I prayed, 'Oh God! Help me and You don't have much time to make up your mind.'"

You and I probably know a lot about "panic prayers." We pray all kinds of panic prayers: "Oh, God, this plane is about to crash—what shall I do?" "Oh, God, my children are on drugs and disobeying me—what shall I do?" "Oh,

Chapter 6: Chariots of Fire

God, my marriage is falling apart—what shall I do?" "Oh, God, my spouse was diagnosed with a terrible illness—what shall I do?"

We know a lot about panic prayers because many of us run scared. We are chronic worriers. We worry about the skeletons of the past, the demands of the present and the insecurities of the future.

The Syrians were making war against the Israelites. It was not an all-out offensive, only skirmishes along the border. The Syrian strategy was this: Whenever they saw a piece of territorial border that was not protected, they attempted to lay claim to it. The problem was that when the Syrians ambushed the area, they were ambushed by the soldiers of Israel.

After this had happened several times, the king of Syria called his generals together and said, "There must be a traitor among us. Someone is telling our plans to the Israelites." Of course, the king's generals denied the charge. They told the king about Elisha: "There is a prophet in Israel who knows every move you make. He tells the king of Israel and he orders his soldiers to the area where you are getting ready to attack. In fact, the prophet hears so clearly from heaven that he even knows what you are saying in your bedroom."

The Syrian king decided that the only thing to do was to send a great army out to apprehend this prophet. Can you imagine a whole army going out to get one man who is not even a soldier but a preacher?

The Syrian scouts discovered that Elisha the prophet was living in Dothan. The Syrians went under the cover of night, surrounded the area and waited until morning. Their plan was to capture the prophet who was causing them so much trouble.

The next morning, the first person out of the house was not Elisha but his servant. The servant looked out and saw the entire Syrian army surrounding them. He was absolutely terrified. He ran back into the house and said to Elisha, "We are surrounded! The Syrian army is here! There is no way out! What shall we do?"

Elisha was not afraid. The prophet knew who was in control of the situation because he completely trusted God. He prayed, "Lord, open his eyes that he may see." The Lord opened the eyes of the young man and saw that "the mountain was full of horses and chariots of fire all around Elisha." The heavenly host was there to protect him from the enemy.

"Oh, God, what shall we do?" I wonder how many times we have said that. We Christians talk a pretty good "faith" game. We preach and teach about faith. We may even do a little bragging about faith. Have you ever heard someone say, "Well, I have all the faith in the world that it will be okay." But when it comes down to the wire we often panic and say, "Oh, God, what shall we do?"

The point is that God's Spirit is present and with us. The "chariots of fire" around Elisha represent the very presence and power of God Himself. God is with His people. God protects His people. God's help is at hand. God surrounds us with chariots of fire. The problem is that our faith wanes in the midst of adversity.

Faith is an intangible. We live in a world that is totally oriented to the physical senses. We want something we can touch, see, hear, taste and smell. We want something we can grab and hold on to. It is difficult for us to imagine that we can touch the "untouchable." Just because you cannot see something does not make it any less real. You cannot see love, but life would be most difficult without it. You cannot see hope, but you would become completely hopeless without it. You cannot see faith, yet you can experience it in your heart. Faith is just as real as love and hope.

The Bible Is Real

First, faith believes that the Bible is a reality. It is God's road map for life. The Psalmist prayed, "Your word is a lamp to my feet and a light to my path" (119:105). No matter how many Bibles you have, they will do you little good unless you read them. "So then faith comes by hearing, and hearing by the word of God" (Romans 10:17).

How are we ever going to be able to enrich our lives with the Christian faith unless we read the Word of God, believe in its truth and put it into practice? The Bible is more than just a book on the shelf or a collectible item to be displayed. It is the inspired Word of God.

A man who was cleaning out his attic had a friend who collected old books. His friend came to see him one evening. The man said, "You know, I thought about you today. I was cleaning out my attic, and I found an old Bible named 'Guten-something,' and I threw it out because it was so old and falling apart." The friend said, "You threw out a Gutenberg Bible!" The man replied, "Don't worry about it. You wouldn't have wanted it. It was marked up by some old bird named Martin Luther."

An explorer discovered an ancient sundial. Recognizing its value, he put it in a museum where it would be shielded from the elements—including the sun. Although he valued it, he never used it.

Unfortunately, too many Christians do the same with the Bible. We see the Bible as valuable but requiring too much effort to understand and apply. We need to remember that the Bible is God's living Word about a living Person who can change us if we let Him. Sundials work only when exposed to the sun. So it is with the Bible. We must read it in the light of God's love for us through His Son Jesus Christ.

Prayer Is Real

Second, faith believes that prayer is a reality. Faith knows that God hears and answers prayer. Prayer does not change God. God changes the one praying through his prayer. Prayer does not change God's mind about a situation. God changes the situation in response to our intercessory prayer. It is not prayer that works. It is God who works through prayer. Sometimes we do not know what to pray or how to pray. Paul says, "We do not know what we should pray for as we ought, but the Spirit Himself makes intercession for us with groanings which cannot be uttered" (Romans 8:26).

Our emergency system in the United States is state-of-the-art. Whenever you dial 911, you are immediately connected to a dispatcher. The dispatcher will see a readout that lists your telephone number, your address, and the name under which your telephone is listed. Also listening in are the police, the fire department and the paramedics.

A caller might not be able to state what the problem is. Perhaps a woman's husband has just suffered a heart attack, and she is so out of control that all she can do is scream into the telephone. But the dispatcher does not need her to say anything. He knows where the call is coming from. Help is on the way.

Times come into our lives when in our desperation, distress or pain, we dial 911 prayers. Sometimes we are hysterical. Sometimes we do not know the words to speak. But God hears and He is present. He knows our name and our circumstances. Through the initiatives of His amazing grace, He dispatches the chariots of fire. Help is on the way.

A Sunday school teacher opened her lesson by asking the question, "Which Bible character would you like to be?" A little girl said, "I would like to be Mary because she was the mother of the baby Jesus." A little boy said, "I would like to be David because he killed Goliath with his sling." Another child said, "I would like to be Joseph because he had a coat of many colors." But it was Little Johnny who said, "I would like to be Lo." The teacher said, "Who is that Bible character?" Johnny answered, "Well, Jesus said, 'Lo, I am with you always.'"

A wealthy woman phoned the manager of a concert hall and asked, "Have you found a diamond pendant? I

Chapter 6: Chariots of Fire

think I lost it in your building last night." The manager replied, "No, we haven't found it, but we'll look. Please hold the line." During a quick search, the valuable diamond was located. When the manager returned to the phone, however, the woman was no longer on the line. She had hung up. She never called again, and the expensive jewelry went unclaimed.

We would fault that woman for her impatience and lack of persistence, but we sometimes act just like that when we pray. And in doing so, we give up something much more precious than diamonds. We lose the opportunity to have the God of the universe help us with our problems, meet our needs or lead us to do His will. Often we hurriedly make our requests but fail to "hold the line."

As Christians we know that God is with us. Emmanuel—"God with us!" God will not desert us. Nothing, not even death, can separate us from Him. Jesus Christ, our Lord, has promised to be with us—no matter what. The chariots of fire are around us. Why? His Holy Spirit is with us.

Dag Hammarskjöld said it so succinctly in his daily prayer:

> Give me a pure heart—that I may see Thee,
> A humble heart—that I may hear Thee,
> A heart of love—that I may serve Thee,
> A heart of faith—that I may abide in Thee.

What on earth will you do for heaven's sake when you take hold of a personal faith and know that God dispatches His chariots of fire to be around you?

Chapter 7

The Power to Choose

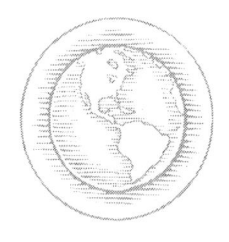

Now faith is the substance of things hoped for, the evidence of things not seen. For by it the elders obtained a good testimony . . . By faith Abraham obeyed when he was called to go out to the place which he would receive as an inheritance. And he went out, not knowing where he was going. By faith he dwelt in the land of promise as in a foreign country, dwelling in tents with Isaac and Jacob, the heirs with him of the same promise; for he waited for the city which has foundations, whose builder and maker is God. By faith Sarah herself also received strength to conceive seed, and she bore a child when she was past the age, because she judged Him faithful who had promised. Therefore from one man, and him as good as dead, were born as many as the stars of the sky in multitude—innumerable as the sand which is by the seashore (Hebrews 11:1–2, 8–12).

The greatest power a person possesses is the power to choose. Think about that for a moment. We make choices everyday that affect our lives. We choose the kind of clothes we wear . . . the kind of car we drive . . . the books we read . . . the church we attend . . . the foods we eat . . . the music we hear . . . the friends we enjoy . . . whom we like and whom we dislike.

We possess the power to choose to be lazy or ambitious, friendly or unfriendly, cooperative or stubborn, exciting or dull, lovable or angry. We can choose to believe that everyone is out to get us, or we can choose to believe that people are inherently good. We can choose to be a winner or we can choose to lay back and do little. We can choose to be positive or we can choose to be negative about life. We can choose to vote or not to vote in a political election.

Many people today are cynical and say, "Why should I get involved? How can my choice to vote or not to vote make a difference in an election?" Just look at history. Did you know that:

> In 1645 one vote gave Oliver Cromwell control of England.
>
> In 1649 one vote caused Charles I of England to be executed.
>
> In 1845 one vote brought Texas into the Union.
>
> In 1868 one vote saved President Andrew Johnson from impeachment.
>
> In 1875 one vote changed France from a monarchy to a republic.
>
> In 1876 one vote gave Rutherford B. Hayes the presidency of the United States.
>
> In 1923 one vote gave Adolf Hitler leadership in the Nazi Party.
>
> In 1941 one vote saved the Selective Service—just weeks before Pearl Harbor.

Chapter 7: The Power to Choose

In 1960 one vote change in each precinct in Illinois would have denied John F. Kennedy the presidency.

The point is that we use or misuse this great power that God has given us. Our attitude about the power of choice separates everyone into two groups of people. Someone once wrote, "It's not the good and the bad, for the good are half-bad and the bad are half-good. Not the happy and sad, for the years bring to each of us our individual shares of laughter and tears. Not the rich and the poor, for if you count a person's wealth you must first know the state of their conscience and health. Still there are just two kinds of people on earth: the people who lift and the people who lean. Strangely enough, you will find on today's scene only one lifter to twenty who lean."

A psychologist put it this way, "There are two types of human beings: those who think of life as a privilege and those who think of it as a problem. The first type is enthusiastic, energetic, resistant to shock and responsive to challenge. The other type is suspicious, hesitant, withholding, and self-centered. To the first group, life is hopeful, exciting. To the second, it's a potential ambush."

We need to understand that the Christian life is more than intellectual assent to some doctrine. It is more than the acknowledgment of a creed. The Christian life is a receiving of Christ by faith into our hearts as Lord and Savior. This choice is so pervasive that it brings a basic reorientation toward life. It is believing in the fact that because God is alive and at work in this world, life can be different and we can make a difference. It is realizing that the Christian faith is an on-going adventure. It is the assurance that God is with us in the present, and because God does forgive and cleanse us from our sins, He is at work in all things for the good of those who love Him. Therefore, what happens to us is not nearly so important as how we respond to what is happening.

Obviously, our lives will not always run smoothly. Life at times is difficult, stressful and fastidious. A first-grade school teacher was having a horrible day. It had rained all day, and thirty-seven first-graders had been cooped up in a small classroom with no recess. The children were wild. She could not get them calmed down. There had been one problem after another all day long. The teacher was beside herself, even more anxious than the children for the bell to ring to close the day.

At 2:45 the teacher noticed it was still raining outside, so she began the task of getting the right raincoats, the right rain hats and the right boots on the right kids. Finally, she had all of them fixed and ready to go home, except for Little Johnny. He had a pair of boots that were impossible to get on. No zippers, no snaps, no hooks—they had to be pulled on with great effort.

The teacher pushed and pulled, yanked and jerked until finally they slipped on. Then Little Johnny said, "Teacher, you know what? These boots ain't mine." The teacher wanted to scream, but she didn't. She said a prayer and kept her cool. She pulled and jerked and yanked, and finally they came off. Then Little Johnny said, "Teacher, they're my sister's, but she lets me wear 'em!"

Our lives will not always run smoothly, but we have the power to choose how we will respond to whatever life throws our way. Likewise, the Christian life is not always a smooth journey.

Abraham left the security of his home country and ventured off into a distant land to become the father of a new people. God spoke to him and said, "Leave this country and go to a place where I will show you." Abraham left his home, Ur of the Chaldees, and moved ahead with no idea of where he was going. When he reached the land of promise, he lived there as though he were in a "strange" country. Ultimately, Abraham was looking for that city whose foundation and architect is God.

Chapter 7: The Power to Choose

We look to Jesus as the pioneer and perfecter of our faith. He is the One we choose to follow on this journey. Still there are choices that we have to make for Christ every day. God has given us freedom to choose whether or not to remain faithful.

If we choose the path of faith, then life truly becomes an adventure. The greatest thrill in the world is to be a part of something that taps your God-given potential and calls you to be your very best—to be who God wants you to be and to be a part of something that is eternal and greater than yourself.

Years ago, in a burst of civic pride, the city of Richmond, Virginia, commissioned a statue of General Robert E. Lee on his horse, Traveler. When the statue arrived on a flat rail car, the citizenry chose to pull the statue to its site. Flags adorned the route. Crowds gathered along the way. The bands played. Rich and poor, leading citizens and poor servants, all pulled together. At the end, someone cut a piece of the rope as a souvenir. The idea quickly spread, and many others did the same thing. Years later citizens of Richmond would say, "I had hold of the rope, did you?"

Our life of faith together in the Body of Christ is a lifelong happening. The harvest of people that God desires to bring to the church is beyond our human expectations. Will you be able to look back on your life and say, "I had hold of the rope of faith in Christ, and I helped to make it happen"? What significant part are you having in the life and ministry of the church?

Ronald E. Osborn put it this way: "Unless you try to do something beyond what you have already mastered, you will never grow. But undertake something that is difficult, and it will do you great good."

Psychologist Rollo May once said, "The clearest picture of the empty life is the suburban man, who gets up at the same hour every weekday morning, takes the same route to work in the city, performs the same task at the office, lunches at the same place, leaves the same tip for the waitress each day, comes home the same route each night, goes to church every Christmas and Easter, and moves through a mechanical existence year after year until he finally retires at sixty-five and very soon thereafter dies of heart failure." Dr. May adds, "And I've always suspected that he dies of boredom."

The gospel tells us there is something more to life. People who choose Christ and give themselves unreservedly to Him will find more meaning and purpose in life. A tepid faith will never be on the cutting edge. With a spirit of timidity we will have difficulty going forward. If we do not choose to go all the way with Jesus, we will never find that "something more" that transforms life and gives it meaning, direction and purpose.

About forty years ago in Burlington, Iowa, a Civil Air Patrol plane went out of control when the pilot twirled the propeller to start the engine. In those days, a pilot cranked his plane by spinning the propeller. It was possible for an unmanned plane to take off on its own once the engine gained speed. And that's exactly what happened. The plane circled over the city of Burlington for an hour. Fire trucks and police cars went throughout the city to warn people of possible danger. School children were not permitted to leave the buildings. Students at the college evacuated the campus. After an hour, the plane climbed to 12,000 feet, headed west and eventually crashed in a cornfield in Illinois when it ran out of gas. For two hours the plane had been without a pilot.

Those who try to keep their lives airborne without a pilot will fail. A faith that would keep us airborne is not merely a set of beliefs in the existence of God or the spark of goodness in human nature. A faith that would save us is not a confidence in human abilities or potential.

The faith that saves us, that keeps us airborne, is a personal faith in a specific person—the person of Jesus Christ.

"It is not I who live," testified Paul, "but Christ Jesus who lives in me." This is the key to a new adventure and the secret to the Spirit-filled life.

As someone has written, "In darkness there is no choice. It is light that enables us to see the difference between things; and it is Christ that gives us light."

What on earth will you do for heaven's sake with the power of choice?

Chapter 8

When King Uzziah Dies

When [Uzziah] was strong his heart was lifted up, to his destruction, for he transgressed against the LORD his God by entering the temple of the LORD to burn incense on the altar of incense. So Azariah the priest went in after him, and with him were eighty priests of the LORD, valiant men. And they withstood King Uzziah, and said to him, "It is not for you, Uzziah, to burn incense to the LORD, but for the priests, the sons of Aaron, who are consecrated to burn incense. Get out of the sanctuary, for you have trespassed! You shall have no honor from the LORD God."

Then Uzziah became furious; and he had a censer in his hand to burn incense. And while he was angry with the priests, leprosy broke out on his forehead, before the priests in the house of the LORD, beside the incense altar. And Azariah the chief priest and all the priests looked at him, and there, on his forehead, he was leprous; so they thrust him out of that place. Indeed he also hurried to get out, because the LORD had struck him.

King Uzziah was a leper until the day of his death. He dwelt in an isolated house, because he was a leper; for he was cut off from the house of the LORD. Then Jotham his son was over the king's house, judging the people of the land.

Now the rest of the acts of Uzziah, from first to last, the prophet Isaiah the son of Amoz wrote. So Uzziah rested with his fathers, and they buried him with his fathers in the field of burial which belonged to the kings, for they said, "He is a leper"
(2 Chronicles 26:16–23).

In the year that King Uzziah died, I saw the LORD sitting on a throne, high and lifted up, and the train of His robe filled the temple (Isaiah 6:1).

· ·

"In the year that King Uzziah died . . ." This is more than a historical chronology of Jewish kings. It is more than a date in biblical history. It is a reminder of the wonderful and mysterious ways that God uses to bring us to Himself.

Uzziah was sixteen years old when he was crowned king of Judah. His reign lasted for fifty-two years. Uzziah's reign was not only long; it was grand and majestic. He was held to be the greatest king since Solomon. National pride was higher than it had been since the Queen of Sheba had knelt at Solomon's feet. Israel extended its sovereignty to increasingly remote borders.

The great King Uzziah took the kingdom of Judah to dazzling heights of material prosperity, military power and national glory. The renowned king had two names—*Uzziah,*

Chapter 8: When King Uzziah Dies

which means "Jehovah His Strength;" and *Azariah*, which means "Jehovah His Helper."

One can imagine how Uzziah's glory must have affected young Isaiah. He was the only king Isaiah had ever known. King Uzziah was young Isaiah's hero, his idol. Uzziah not only sat upon the throne of the palace but on the throne of Isaiah's heart. Isaiah's hopes and dreams for the nation and his own life were wrapped up in the power and glory of the king.

Unfortunately, Uzziah's reign had begun in faithfulness and obedience to God but ended in shame and humiliation. The Scripture says that when Uzziah "was strong his heart was lifted up, to his destruction" (2 Chronicles 26:16). In his arrogance he thought he could take the place of the priests. He thought he could dispense with God's appointed ways and do anything he pleased. So he took shortcuts and circumvented the laws of God.

One day he entered the temple and rushed into the Holy Place where only a priest was allowed to go. The king, not the priest, would offer his own sacrifice to the Lord. But when he came out, he was no longer a proud and glorious king. Uzziah staggered out a leper—broken, humiliated and unclean, "because the LORD had struck him."

King Uzziah was forced to move out of the palace, and from that time on he lived according to the strict Jewish laws governing lepers. The king of Israel, the greatest since Solomon, became an outcast living in a place of quarantine and social separation.

Can you imagine what this did to young Isaiah's heart? His great king, his hero, was now a quarantined leper. Surely God would heal him and restore him to his throne. But the Chronicler says "King Uzziah was a leper until the day of his death. He dwelt in an isolated house, because he was a leper; for he was cut off from the house of the LORD" (2 Chronicles 26:21).

What a blow this must have been to young Isaiah! King Uzziah, the mightiest monarch since King Solomon, was dead. And he died as a leper! The one on whom Isaiah had pinned his hopes and dreams died in disgrace.

In the year that King Uzziah died, two thrones were actually emptied—the throne in the palace of the king and the throne of young Isaiah's heart. This emptying was essential if Isaiah were to experience the living God. The throne of his heart had to be emptied before he could see God "sitting on a throne." His false god had to be brought down before he could see the true God "high and lifted up." In one sense, Isaiah had to come to the end of himself before he could make a new beginning of life with God.

The point is that we usually have to go through the deep surgery of detachment from every idolatrous attachment in order to empty the thrones of our hearts. Only then can God fill them. False gods must come down before we can see the true God high and lifted up.

Often we do not seek after God earnestly and sincerely until we have tried many things in life and found only emptiness. Most of the time this does not happen naturally or easily. It often results from great crisis. Only when we reach the place of utter desperation, when we have exhausted all human resources, do we turn to God. When our "Uzziah" dies, when our idol is broken, when we face disillusion, then we turn our eyes toward God. Our extremity becomes God's opportunity.

A man related a difficult experience he had gone through. The familiar routines of his life were rudely disturbed. His dreams lay shattered. His lifestyle changed drastically. His future was threatened. Yet this became the means of his seeing himself in a truly lost condition. Through this experience he found Jesus as Savior. He testified: "It was those blessed jolts that brought me face-to-face with my need for God."

A brilliant student was so sure of himself that he felt he had no need for God. His eyes were blinded and his ears were deaf to any awareness of God. Then one day he was jolted out of his self-reliance. His world fell apart overnight. He began to ask questions. He went through a deep soul-searching experience. Jesus Christ Himself went to him and answered his questions. An entirely new purpose became his. His name was Saul, and his jolt on the Damascus Road changed the very course of history.

A certain businessman made a fortune and had everything money could buy. Then overnight his business investments changed. He lost his fortune and was reduced to bankruptcy. He almost lost his mind and even attempted suicide. In the crisis that followed his financial ruin, Jesus Christ changed his life. In the year that his bank account was emptied, his heart was filled with God. He was jolted out of the idolatry of gold and silver into the worship of God.

There was a fine young couple from Christian homes. Their Christian faith was the "inherited" variety. They had no real experience of the living Christ. They tried to fill their inner emptiness with love for one another. They looked to their marriage and love for each other to fulfill all their needs and solve all their problems. After a few years of living in disillusionment their communication began to break down. He began to clam up and she began to nag. They lived together in marital loneliness.

Men and women make good husbands and wives if they work hard at it, but they make lousy gods. In the year their marriage died they saw the Lord high and lifted up, and their marriage took on a new meaning and purpose.

In the year that the temporary and transient passed away, Isaiah discovered the eternal and everlasting God. In the year that every dream was shattered Isaiah discovered reality. In the year that everything fell apart and changed, Isaiah discovered the God who never changes. In the year that King Uzziah died, Isaiah discovered the King of kings.

In 1934 in South Africa, the great Yonker's diamond was discovered. It weighed 726 carats—one of the largest diamonds ever discovered. As it was, however, it was of little value. In 1935 the owner asked Laser Kaplan, the greatest diamond cutter in the world, to cut the diamond into twelve great stones. Kaplan spent a year studying the 726-carat gem. One wrong stroke would shatter it. In 1936 with confidence, firmness and precision he split the diamond into twelve beautiful gems—by his taps and jolts.

God is in the diamond-cutting business. We are like diamonds in the rough. God sees our potential to become jewels in His crown. He has marvelous plans for us.

What on earth will you do for heaven's sake when your King Uzziah dies?

Chapter 9

The Gospel According to You

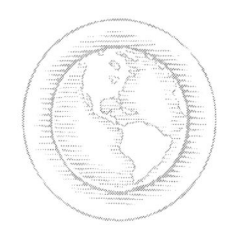

When the south wind blew softly, supposing that they had obtained their desire, putting out to sea, they sailed close by Crete. But not long after, a tempestuous head wind arose, called Euroclydon. So when the ship was caught, and could not head into the wind, we let her drive. And running under the shelter of an island called Clauda, we secured the skiff with difficulty. When they had taken it on board, they used cables to undergird the ship; and fearing lest they should run aground on the Syrtis Sands, they struck sail and so were driven. And because we were exceedingly tempest-tossed, the next day they lightened the ship. On the third day we threw the ship's tackle overboard with our own hands. Now when neither sun nor stars appeared for many days, and no small tempest beat on us, all hope that we would be saved was finally given up.

But after long abstinence from food, then Paul stood in the midst of them and said, "Men, you should have listened to me, and not have sailed from Crete and incurred this disaster and loss. And now I urge you to take heart, for there will be no loss of life among you, but only of the ship. For there stood by me this night an angel of the God to whom I belong and whom I serve, saying, 'Do not be afraid, Paul; you must be brought before Caesar; and indeed God has granted you all those who sail with you.' Therefore take heart, men, for I believe God that it will be just as it was told me" (Acts 27:13–25).

· ·

Someone went to his minister on one occasion and said, "Preacher, which one of the Gospels is read the most—Matthew, Mark, Luke or John?" The minister replied, "Why, none of these! The gospel that is read and seen the most is the gospel according to you. Your actions, your reactions, your attitudes, what you say and the things you do describes the gospel according to you."

The gospel according to the Apostle Paul was a wonderful gospel. On many occasions, he was able to proclaim his faith. One of the incidences is found in Acts 27. He was able to take authority and declare what he believed as the man of faith that he had become. Paul said, "So take heart, men, for I have faith in God that it will be exactly as I have been told."

Through the adversity of a shipwreck, Paul had a wonderful opportunity to declare the gospel as he understood it. The gospel according to Paul was to share the good news of what Jesus had done in his life and how He could work in their lives.

When they landed on the shore, they were all soaking wet. They were disabled in every way. But it wasn't long until Paul, a prisoner, established himself as the man who was the true leader. Before long, people from all over the

Chapter 9: The Gospel According to You

island of Malta were bringing their diseases and troubles to him. Paul began to do a mighty work in the name of Jesus. The gospel according to Paul, through his actions and attitudes, words and deeds, and his stance in life even though a prisoner, was making a tremendous witness for Jesus Christ.

The question is straightforward: What is the gospel according to you?

Alumni of Wheaton College had gathered at a class reunion reminiscing about the good old days. One of the people remarked, "I remember Dr. Cook driving down the street, and I saw him stop and get out of the car. A little boy was trying to reach inside a mailbox and could not. Dr. Cook went to his assistance. He lifted the little boy up so he could get the mail." That's the gospel according to this college professor.

A high school senior who had received Jesus as Savior and Lord said to his pastor, "I can't find a job in town, but I've found a job in the northern woods of Maine. I'm going up there to work in a lumber yard." The preacher replied, "Oh, I don't know if that would be spiritually wise. They are liable to make fun of your Christian witness." The young Christian replied, "Oh, don't worry about me. I'll be fine." When he came back in the early fall, the preacher noticed he was back in church. "Well, how was it in the woods of Maine? How did you get along in your faith?" asked the preacher. The young man said, "I got along just fine. They didn't ask me, and I didn't tell them." That's the gospel according to this high school senior.

During the Vietnam War, a company of soldiers came under heavy fire. Two men went out on the point. One was killed and the other was seriously wounded. After they'd been pinned down for hours, a soldier crawled under heavy enemy fire to save his comrade. Instead of staying in the safety and security of the foxhole, the soldier went to assist his buddy. When he reached him, his friend spoke a few words and then died.

The soldier pulled the body of his fallen comrade back to his company under heavy enemy fire. In the process he, too, was wounded in the side. His commanding officer said, "You fool! Why did you risk your life to save a dead soldier?" The wounded soldier replied, "Because when I got to him he said, "I knew you would come." That soldier was willing to do whatever it took to reach his friend. As Christians we are to have the same sacrificial spirit that reaches out to bring others to the salvation that is available in Jesus Christ.

Patrick Henry's last will and testament read: "I have now disposed of all my property to my family. There is one thing more I wish I could give them and that is faith in Jesus Christ. If they had that and I had not given them one shilling, they would have been rich; and if they had not that, and I had given them the world, they would be poor indeed."

What is the gospel according to you? What gospel have people read from your life today? What you do in every moment is a part of the gospel according to you—through your words, attitudes, courtesies and actions. Someone once said, "To live with a saint in heaven will be a thing of glory, but to live with a saint on earth is quite another story." How does your life impact others for Christ? This is the will of God in Christ Jesus—the gospel according to you.

Dr. John McFerrin was General Braxton Bragg's chaplain in the Confederate Army. One chilly day in November as he walked over a battlefield near Chattanooga, he read to the dying soldiers from his Bible as they lay bleeding on the field. He said to a wounded soldier, "Let me read to you." "Oh, Chaplain," said the soldier, "I am so thirsty; I am so thirsty." John McFerrin ran to the nearest water he could find. Pouring some in his hat, he carried it to the soldier and pressed the water to his lips. "Now, brother, let me read to you." "Oh, Chaplain, I am so cold." The chaplain took his light overcoat and put it around the wounded man, touching him as tenderly as a mother would her baby. The soldier looked up into the face of McFerrin and said, "Now,

Chapter 9: The Gospel According to You

Chaplain, if there is anything in that book that makes a Rebel chaplain treat a Yankee soldier this way, read it to me."

A little boy knelt beside his bed and prayed, "Dear God, help me to be like my daddy, so fun to be with, patient and kind, strong and dependable, firm but fair, and Christlike in every way." The father knelt beside his bed and prayed, "Dear God, help me to be like my son, honest and true, eager to learn, full of energy, ready to obey, and trusting in every way."

What is the gospel according to you as a parent? Are you living in such a way that your children want to be like you? Do they see Jesus Christ in your life? You know that they pick up on every attitude and action they see in you.

We display the gospel by the life we lead. The gospel according to you will determine the future of your church, the way life will be transformed, the moral character of your community and the quality of your family life. Someone once wrote the following:

> If none but you in the world today
> Had tried to live in a Christlike way,
> Could the rest of the world look close at you
> And find the path that is straight and true?
> If none but you in the world so wide
> Had found the Christ for his daily guide,
> Would the things you do and the things you say
> Lead others to live in His blessed way?
> Ah, friends of the Christ, in the world today
> Are many, who watch you upon your way,
> And look to the things you say and do
> To measure the Christian standard true!
> But what do they say and what do they think
> Of the gospel according to you?
> You are writing each day a letter to all—
> Take care that the writing is true;
> 'Tis the only Gospel that some will read,
> That Gospel according to you.

A blind Englishmen was noted for a lantern he always carried. People often asked, "What use is the lantern to you, since you are blind?" The wise old man replied, "I do not carry it to prevent my stumbling over others but to keep them from stumbling over me." Herein lies the challenge of the Christian faith we profess. Let us make certain that no one stumbles because the faith we profess and the faith we practice are so different.

God is counting on you to be a part of his work in the church. Unless you give expression to the gospel, the gospel goes unspoken. Unless you live out the gospel, the gospel will not be noticed. Unless you take a stand for Jesus, there is liable to be no one taking a stand.

What on earth will you do for heaven's sake with the gospel according to you?

Chapter 10

Spiritual Seasons of the Soul

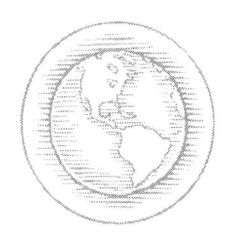

*To everything there is a season, A time for every
purpose under heaven: A time to be born,
And a time to die; A time to plant,
And a time to pluck what is planted; A time to kill,
And a time to heal; A time to break down,
And a time to build up; A time to weep,
And a time to laugh; A time to mourn,
And a time to dance; A time to cast away stones,
And a time to gather stones; A time to embrace,
And a time to refrain from embracing; A time to gain,
And a time to lose; A time to keep,
And a time to throw away; A time to tear,
And a time to sew; A time to keep silence,
And a time to speak; A time to love,
And a time to hate; A time of war,
And a time of peace (Ecclesiastes 3:1–8).*

This passage in Ecclesiastes is the microcosm of human life. It applies to all things related to you and to me. God has established the seasons of life: "To everything there is a season, a time for every purpose under heaven." Just as there are four seasons in the calendar year, so there are spiritual seasons of the soul.

There is not just one season in this world. There are four distinct seasons. These seasons have continued from the time God created the heavens and the earth. The Scripture declares that they will continue to go on through the eons. The point is that these seasons correlate with human life.

Any episode in your life has a season to it. There is a season that brings it in and a season that bids it farewell. For every event in your life there is a season. There is a time to be born and a time to die. There is a time to plant and a time to pluck up what is planted. There is a time *to work,* a time *to wait,* a time *to reap* and a time *to rest.*

Everything in existence goes through seasons. The entire created order is going through changes or phases. This involves our physical bodies, our social interactions, our families, our marriages and our churches. As someone has succinctly said, "What goes around—comes around." Everything is in the process of change. Everything is in a state of flux. In his God-given wisdom, Solomon is exactly right: Everything under the sun has its season.

Just as there are natural seasons in the created order, so there are spiritual seasons in the Christian life. Unless we know what season our life is in, we will never grasp the joy of the Lord and God's purpose for us. There are certain things we need to know about the season we are in.

If we ever get to the point that we want only the warmth and beauty of the spring season, and the other seasons are viewed as something to endure, then we will miss seventy-five percent of God's purpose for us. Someone has written:

Chapter 10: Spiritual Seasons of the Soul

It was spring, but it was summer I wanted; the warm days and the great outdoors.
It was summer, but it was fall I wanted; the colorful leaves and the cool, dry air.
It was fall, but it was winter I wanted; the beautiful snow and the joyful holiday season.
I was a child, but it was adulthood I wanted; the freedom and respect it brings.
I was twenty, but it was thirty I wanted; to be mature and sophisticated.
I was middle-aged, but it was twenty I wanted; the youth and the free spirit.
I was retired, but it was middle-aged I wanted; the presence of mind, and without limitations.
My life was over and I never got what I wanted.

We often live life this way. No season is more important than another season. Some are more enjoyable, but no one particular season is more important than another. They are all necessary over the course of life.

Springtime is a time to plan and work. When spring comes, people start working in their yards. We begin to plant and garden in the springtime. You start with a plan and you work your plan. You till the soil and plant certain things at a certain depth. You water and fertilize. You cultivate the soil and separate the weeds from the plants and shrubs. Then the summer season comes.

Summertime is a time to watch and wait. Summertime is a time of great growth and increase. Your plants begin to grow. The blossoms come into view with their buds and flowers. People start picking the flowers and say, *"This is beautiful. This is what I want!"* But if they pick their blossoms prematurely, they will lose their fruit. You have to wait. You have to be patient. You see the evidence of growth, but you dare not interfere with what God has ordained. Then, the autumn season comes.

Autumn is a time for reaping the harvest. This is when you get paid for the labor you did in the spring. This is the season when you gather the fruit. The autumn is a time for the harvest.

We can become so euphoric about the springtime, the summertime and the autumn that we forget another season is coming. In the next season, not much is going on. But this season is just as important as the other three. It is the wintertime season.

Wintertime gives the appearance of death, defeat and despair. When winter comes, everything looks gray and gloomy. But things continue to live in the wintertime. All may appear dead, but they are very much alive. Life goes through its appointed seasons. Now it is wintertime. In fact, life cannot recover from the springtime, the summertime and the harvest without the wintertime. There must be a time of rest and refreshment. Some plants cannot produce next year unless they go through a cold, hard wintertime.

While the summertime is full of activity and the limbs are reaching upward toward heaven with blossoms, the wintertime is when the root goes down. The limbs do not go up. But the root structure spreads and gets deeper. The foundation becomes stronger and more stable. The roots grow deeper and become more entrenched.

Wintertime is often equated with gloominess. Many of the beautiful plants you see growing outside were growing in the wintertime. But in the wintertime, they were just growing in a different direction. They were growing down and getting deeper. There is wintertime in our spiritual walk with Jesus.

Some want to live only in the activity of the summertime. Many people love the summertime—when everything seems to be just right and enjoyable. There are those who want to be only on the mountaintop of springtime. They love the springtime—when everything runs smoothly and is so beautiful.

Chapter 10: Spiritual Seasons of the Soul

We cannot live life in only one or two seasons. God knows it, and He has designed our lives in such a way that when we have exhausted ourselves with activity or bearing fruit, He allows us to come to a period of isolation and weariness. The reason is so that we can be refurbished and restored for the next springtime and the harvest that comes in autumn.

If you are in the wintertime of your soul, Jesus has not forsaken you. It is not that you have messed up or done something wrong. It is the Lord loving you enough to work His Spirit deeper in you. It is the Lord giving you rest, so He can prepare you for a greater experience and a deeper knowledge in Him. It is the Lord allowing your faith to increase. It is the Lord loving you enough to allow your roots to grow deeper in Him.

In the summertime, you are doing something for the Lord. But in the wintertime God is doing something for you. In the summertime, you are busy with activity. But in the wintertime, God's Spirit is busy with His activity in you.

The human heart is like a garden. God is nurturing and caring for the fruit that will burst forth from your life. He is cultivating His life in your soul. He wants you to bear fruit in the springtime of your spiritual life and to do it in even greater proportions.

Every time God did something great through Elijah, that event was preceded by a time of isolation, depression and hunger. Remember when the Lord led Elijah to the Brook Cherith? While he was there, the ravens fed him and he drank the branch water. He felt depressed and isolated from society. Only the hand of the Lord fed him. Yet, that wintertime season of his soul led him to go into town and Elijah raised a boy from the dead. While he was in that boy's home, the scripture says that God moved upon a woman to feed Elijah. It came from the hand of the Lord, but He used this woman.

Then God sent Elijah to Mount Carmel. There, he called lightning down from heaven and defeated 450 prophets of

Baal. Elijah had already been through the spring, the summer and the autumn of his spiritual life. And now he was empty again. He was spiritually dry and depleted. He was depressed. He ran from Queen Jezebel and lay down under a Juniper tree and said, "I'm ready to die. I do not know what is wrong with me. Nobody understands me. I'm all by myself. I'm used up and depleted." And God said, "You are exactly where I want you. This is the wintertime of your spiritual walk with me." God allowed Elijah to rest. God woke him up and fed him. The point is this: Just before God did something great through this man, God allowed wintertime to come to his soul. Elijah felt like giving up. He was isolated. But God took care of Elijah, and his roots in the faithfulness of the Lord grew deeper while he was in the wintertime of his soul.

God led Elijah up on the mountain and Elijah discovered something he never knew before about the Lord. He discovered that God did not always speak in the thunder and lightning. He did not always respond with noise or a big bang. Elijah heard God speak in a still small voice.

You and I are no different. We can live only so long in the euphoric heat of the summertime. We can work only so hard in the labor of the springtime. We can harvest only so long in the autumn. That is why our souls need the wintertime.

In China a certain kind of bamboo tree is indigenous to the central mainland. When the Chinese plant the little sprig in the ground, it is not very high. They fertilize and cultivate it very carefully. In the first year, it does not appear to grow an inch. In the second year, they continue to fertilize and cultivate it. There is no measurable growth. Three years pass and it still does not appear to be growing. Four years pass and it nearly looks the same as it did when they first planted it. But in the fifth year, and in a five-week period, it grows ninety feet high.

The question is this: Did it grow ninety feet in five weeks, or did it grow ninety feet in five years? It takes five years to lay a foundation. It takes five years for the roots to go down deep enough to support a bamboo stalk ninety feet into the air. It takes five years to work the cultivation and to watch carefully. Then, when the time is right and the roots are deep enough, it shoots high into the heavens.

Too many of us work at something for maybe four years, and then we decide to do something else because our life is too short. This could be the situation in marriage or in business. All these years you have worked and cultivated that relationship with your spouse or children. All these years you have knocked and made calls, hoping to build up your business. All these years you have served the Lord and you don't understand why. The result is that you feel like giving up. In one sense, you could be at the beginning of the fifth year—in your home, your marriage, your business and your church.

Don't quit in the wintertime. This is the time when God is doing something on the inside. The springtime is just around the corner.

You may be in the wintertime of your marriage, business, career or schooling. Whatever the situation Jesus Christ is with you, regardless of the season.

This is not the day or the time to quit. You are being tested. In the midst of your busyness for God He has been active in you. Your springtime may be close at hand. It is time to plan and to work that plan for Him.

Paul wrote to the church at Galatia, "Let us not grow weary while doing good, for in due season we shall reap if we do not lose heart. Therefore, as we have opportunity, let us do good to all, especially to those who are of the household of faith" (6:9–10).

What on earth will you do for heaven's sake with your spiritual seasons of the soul?

Chapter 11

The Laws of Light

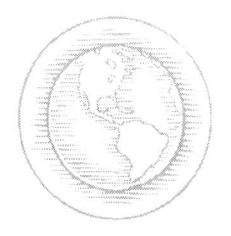

*John 8:12; Matthew 5:14; John 1:5 Jesus spoke . . .
again, saying, "I am the light of the world. He who
follows Me shall not walk in darkness, but have the
light of life (John 8:12).
You are the light of the world. A city that is set on a
hill cannot be hidden (Matthew 5:14).
And the light shines in the darkness, and the darkness
did not comprehend it (John 1:5).*

. . . .

The sun is the source of all light and energy on earth. All physical light in our world comes from the sun as it interacts with the planets, moons and stars in our solar system.

Three basic physical laws govern the origin and transmission of light: Light has a common source, light can be redirected from its source by process of reflection and light is indestructible.

An extrapolation from these physical laws to spiritual laws will be helpful and insightful to the Christian life. Three relevant passages of Scripture parallel these laws of light.

Jesus said, "I am the light of the world" (John 8:12). Jesus said, "You are the light of the world" (Matthew 5:14). Jesus said, "The light shines in the darkness, and the darkness did not comprehend [overcome] it," (John 1:5).

The Source of All True Light

The first spiritual law is that Jesus Christ is the source of all true light. Jesus said, "I am the light of the world." Jesus Christ is the Incarnate Son of God. Jesus has uniquely revealed the nature of God. If we want to know what God is like, then we need to look at Jesus. Jesus said, "I and My Father are one" and "I am in the Father and the Father [is] in me," (John 10:30; 14:11).

More than anyone else, Jesus Christ helps us to understand who God really is and the purpose of His Love: "God was in Christ reconciling the world to Himself," (2 Corinthians 5:19). To know Jesus, is to know God; to believe in Jesus, is to believe in God; and to receive Jesus, is to receive God.

The Church Is the Reflection of Christ's Light

The second spiritual law is that the church is the reflection of Christ's light. Jesus said, "You are the light of the world." The church has often been called the Lighthouse. It is our responsibility to reflect the Light that has graciously been given to us. The church is not the light itself, but the reflection of the true Light.

Just outside Cairo, Egypt, is a place called the Giza plateau. On top of this dusty, desert area stand the three Great Pyramids: Cheops, Chephrum and Mycerinus. The Cheops pyramid is the largest of all and stands at 455 feet high and 750 feet long on each side. Approximately 250,000 blocks of stone weighing from three to ten tons each—a total of over five million tons. The base covers between 13 and 14 acres. This was the burial place for Pharoah Cheops. Upon entering this unbelievable structure, the guide explains the process the ancient Egyptians used to light the interior. They brought light in from the outside by an intricate and extensive system of mirrors. Thus, the workers were able to see how to work on the inside.

Light can be redirected from its source by process of reflection. "You are the light of the world." It is our purpose to reflect the light of Christ in a dark world.

When I was a student at Elon College, some of the guys in the dormitory decided to go camping out in the woods. An abandoned shack on private acreage stood near the campus. The path leading to the cabin was full of stumps and snags. We had a flashlight to help us see the way. In the middle of the night, as we finally settled down to get some sleep, someone outside the cabin fired a shotgun up in the air. We quickly got up, dashed out of the cabin, and ran down the path—without that flashlight. I stumbled over many snags and stumps as I tried to get back to the campus.

I learned something that night. We cannot travel in a world of snags and stumps unless we have a light on our path. In spite of its imperfections, the church is the light of Christ in a darkened world.

Early Christians were called saints. This word does not have the same definition in our day that it had in the early church. The best definition of "saint" I have ever come across is simply: "A person who makes it easy to believe in God." Our relationship with Jesus is to have that personal, intimate dimension.

I heard of a little boy who had deformed legs at birth. For so many years, the little boy could not walk. Finally, through the help of a social worker, he received physical therapy and eventually was able to walk. After about two years, he was able to engage in sports like the rest of the boys. Years later, the social worker shared her experiences with the boy. She said, "Guess where he is now." Her friends suggested he was probably a doctor, lawyer, dentist or minister. The social worker replied, "No, I'm sorry to say that he is not any of those things. He is in jail for a terrible crime." She confessed, "I was so busy teaching him *how* to walk that I forgot to teach him *where* to walk."

We are called to reflect light on the pathway of life so people will understand and see *where* to walk. It is not enough for you alone to know where to walk. Jesus said, "You are the light of the world," and we are to light the pathway for others.

God Cannot Be Defeated and His Church Is Indestructible

The third spiritual law of light is that Christ cannot be defeated and His church is indestructible. "The light shines in the darkness, and the darkness has not overcome it." Jesus said: "I will build My church, and the gates of Hades shall not prevail against it" (Matthew 16:18).

A proverb says: "All the darkness in the world cannot put out a single candle." This means that darkness is at the mercy of light. Light is never at the mercy of darkness.

Daily headlines and the news is often discouraging and depressing. One wonders what tomorrow will bring. But Jesus said, "Do not worry about tomorrow, for tomorrow will worry about its own things" (Matthew 6:34). The light will shine and the darkness will not hinder it.

Joseph Butler was a priest in the Church of England. The highest official on the ecclesiastical ladder was forced to retire due to illness. Queen Anne offered Butler the position. He refused the promotion. In the letter he said; "The church is dying; it's too late to do anything. There is nothing that can

Chapter 11: The Laws of Light

be done." Ten years after he wrote that letter, a young man began his ministry. His faith brought new life, hope and zeal to the Christians of his time. The "spiritual awakening" that resulted has had a ripple effect down to this moment. His name was John Wesley.

You and I cannot put out the light. The news media cannot put out the light. The problems of society cannot put out the light. It is God's light! It is eternal and it is here to stay. We are called to be reflectors of or witnesses to the light. Therefore, everything we do or say has the potential either to reveal or conceal the light of Christ.

Years ago in Scotland, the Clark family had a dream. Clark and his wife worked and saved, making plans for their nine children and themselves to travel to the United States. It had taken years, but they had finally saved enough money and had passports and reservations for the whole family on a new liner to America.

The family was filled with anticipation and excitement about their new life. However, seven days before their departure, a dog bit the youngest son. The doctor sewed up the boy but hung a yellow sheet on the Clark's front door. Because of the possibility of rabies, they were quarantined for fourteen days.

The family dream was dashed. They would not be able to make the trip to America as they had planned. The father, filled with disappointment and anger, walked to the dock to watch the ship leave. The father shed tears of disappointment and cursed both his son and God for their misfortune.

Five days later, the tragic news spread throughout Scotland—the mighty *Titanic* had sunk. The Clark family was to have been on that ship, but because a dog had bitten the son, they were left behind in Scotland.

When Mr. Clark heard the news, he hugged his son and thanked him for saving the family. He thanked God for saving their lives and turning a disappointment into a blessing.

Regardless of the circumstances and the disappointments in life, you and I need to let our light shine. We can let our light shine only if the Holy Spirit abides in us. How bright is the light shining in your life? Does any obstacle block the light from shining? Is the presence of the Holy Spirit continuous? Is your life so transparent that the light of Jesus radiates regardless of the circumstances?

Let us be grateful that we do not live in a world of total darkness and that we do not walk alone. The true Light of the world is Jesus Christ. He is the One who lights the pathway of life and who has called us to be reflectors of that light to bring hope, joy and peace to a world living in darkness.

What on earth will you do for heaven's sake with the laws of light?

Chapter 12

Where Are You?

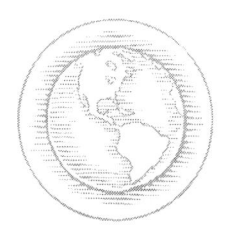

[Adam and Eve] heard the sound of the LORD God walking in the garden in the cool of the day, and Adam and his wife hid themselves from the presence of the LORD God among the trees of the garden. Then the LORD God called to Adam and said to him, "Where are you?" (Genesis 3:8–9).

Little Johnny and his father went to the opera for the first time. The conductor waved the baton and the soprano began her aria. Johnny watched everything intently and finally asked, "Why is he trying to hit her with his stick?" "He's not hitting her," answered his father with a chuckle. "Well then," asked Johnny, "why is she screaming?" We also need to ask ourselves some basic questions.

Where are you in your personal relationship with Jesus Christ today? Through the presence of His Holy Spirit, Jesus is asking each one of us, "Where are you?" We may try to dodge this question or even hide behind a bush. But God knows the secrets of every heart. If we are open and truthful, our answers will indicate where we are in our relationship with Him.

The New Birth

Where are you in the new birth? This is perhaps the most crucial question of all. Suppose you were to die today and stand before God and he were to ask you, "Why should I let you into heaven?" What would your answer be? Some people might not say anything. Others might say: "Well, I've tried to do the best I can. I've tried to live by the Golden Rule, and I've even kept the Ten Commandments." Your "goodness" will not get you into heaven. Only Jesus Christ can do this. Salvation is His gift. It cannot be earned, nor do we deserve it: ". . . by grace you have been saved through faith, and this is not of yourselves, it is the gift of God" (Ephesians 2:8).

Nicodemus was a Pharisee; therefore, he was a "religious" person. He was a "ruler of the Jews"; therefore, he had "social prestige." Nicodemus was wealthy; therefore, he had great "material possessions." From the world's point of view, Nicodemus had it all. Being dissatisfied with his life, he went to Jesus searching for new life that only Jesus could give him.

Jesus told Nicodemus that a man must be born again. He misunderstood Jesus' statement. After all, he was a good, moral, religious person. He fasted two days a week. He spent two hours a day in the Temple praying. He tithed his income on a regular basis. If a pastor-parish committee were seeking the most qualified person they could get for their local church, they would seek someone like Nicodemus. But Jesus said, "All your religious piety and good works are not enough; you must be born again." Nicodemus needed that life that only Jesus Christ can give.

Paul said, "If you confess with your mouth the Lord Jesus and believe in your heart that God has raised Him from the dead, you will be saved. For with the heart one believes unto righteousness, and with the mouth confession is made unto salvation . . . whoever calls on the name of the LORD shall be saved" (Romans 10:9–10, 13).

The new birth is not a reformation but a divine transformation of the totality of life. People are always making resolutions to do better, to change their ways of living or to quit certain habits, but most resolutions are soon broken. Hear how the Scriptures describe the conversion experience when we are born again: from darkness to light; from death to life; from unrighteousness to His righteousness; from stranger to citizen in His kingdom; from orphan to adopted child. The Scriptures teach and affirm that the person who is born again has a changed will, objectives, attitudes and new purpose for life. For it is Jesus who miraculously transforms the old nature into a new creation.

Single-Minded for Christ

Where are you in your single-mindedness for Christ? Paul wrote to the Philippian church: "Let this mind be in you, which was also in Christ Jesus" (2:5). James said: "A double-minded man is unstable in all his ways" (1:8, KJV). A "double-mind" may be glancing at Christ, but it is gazing on something else. Is your mind focused on Christ? Jesus said: "No one can serve two masters; for either he will hate the one and love the other, or else he will be loyal to the one and despise the other" (Matthew 6:24). We either serve the Lord or ourselves. We either cling to Jesus or reject Him.

One of the best examples of what happens to those whose mind is not fixed on God is the children of Israel. When Moses led them out of Egypt, things were not so smooth as they had originally hoped. They began to grumble about the manna, and their grumbling turned toward Moses. But their grumbling was not really against Moses but against God.

A song says it well: "In country, town or city, some people can be found—who spend their lives in grumbling at everything around. Oh yes, they always grumble no matter what we say. They are chronic grumblers and they grumble night and day. They grumble in the city, they grumble on the farm, they grumble at their neighbor, they think it is no harm. They grumble at their husbands, they grumble at their wives, they grumble at their children, but the grumbler never thrives. They grumble when it's raining, they grumble when it's dry, and if the crops are failing they grumble with a sigh. They grumble at the prices, and they grumble if they're high. They grumble all the year around, and they grumble till they die."

Does that describe you? Is your mind focused on Christ? If your mind is not set on the Lord, will you not become a chronic grumbler? Be honest, for God already knows.

Your Devotional Life

Where are you in your devotional life? Where are you in studying the Scriptures? Where are you in your prayer life? Are you making a deliberate effort to learn God's Word? If you are a citizen of God's kingdom, you need to learn and know your rights, duties, privileges and responsibilities so that you can enjoy the full scope of God's blessings.

Too many Christians choose to remain as infantile. Paul had this problem with the Corinthian church: ". . . I, brethren, could not speak to you as spiritual people, but as to carnal, as to babes in Christ. I fed you with milk and not with solid food; for until now you were not ready to receive it; and even now, you are still not able" (1 Corinthians 3:1–2).

When my daughter, Shalen, was about two years old, she was absolutely precious with her baby ways and sounds.

Chapter 12: Where Are You?

If you could have seen her then, you would know what I mean. But if you saw her today at her current age of twenty years old and if she still had her baby ways, you would think that something was terribly wrong with her.

Does your spiritual diet consist of "milk" or "meat"? God is not likely to use the babes as much as He seeks and uses those who are "going on to perfection."

If we say we are following Jesus, one of the places we will follow Him is through the portals of prayer. If we want to fellowship with the Lord in a personal and intimate way, we must spend time with Him and Him alone. We need a daily appointment with God. Whatever is your best time of day, give that to God. If we have time to watch television and read the paper, we certainly have time for God.

Johnny's mother gave him two dimes; one was for the offering and one was to spend as he pleased. Walking down the street feeling wealthy and affluent, he tossed one of the dimes into the air. He miscalculated the catch and saw the coin roll into a drain. Johnny was sad for a moment. He then brightened up and said, "Sorry, Lord, I guess I lost your dime." Does God get our best or only what is leftover?

E. Stanley Jones said, "Most of the casualties in the spiritual life are found at the place of a weakened prayer life. If prayer fades, power fades." Too little prayer and too little Bible reading result in Christians becoming spiritual dwarfs.

God does not call us to a devotional time but to a devotional life. There is certainly nothing wrong with a quiet time. There is a danger in the quiet time becoming nothing more than a nod to God. Make sure that your quiet time has a back door—that it connects with the rest of life.

Study the Scriptures. Learn all you can about your spiritual inheritance through the Scriptures and the tenets of the faith. Pray daily and in everything give thanks to God, for this is the will of Christ Jesus.

Your Service to Christ and to His Church

Where are you in your service to Christ and to His church? We are saved to serve, not to lie in a rest home. James said: ". . . faith by itself, if it does not have works, is dead" (2:17).

From time to time, we need to remind ourselves that Jesus has saved us to serve Him and others. The truth is that many of us have applied a "domestic" mentality to the work and ministry of the church. We think, "Well, I have done my part and I will do no more." If the Sunday school is not growing, why? If the church is not receiving new members and winning people to Christ, why? If there is spiritual sluggishness in your own life, why?

John Wesley said that our chief business is to save souls, calling people to repentance and sharing the saving grace and love of our Lord Jesus Christ. Whenever we complete a task, we should never claim that we have done more than we should. When we look at the cross of Jesus Christ, our greatest offerings of service are only small gifts of gratitude to Him.

The Dead Sea is the lowest point on the face of the earth, 1,291 feet below sea level. The main source of its water comes from the Jordan River. But one of the unique characteristics about the Dead Sea is the absence of biological life. The reason this body of water is dead is because it has no outlet. The Jordan River and all the other tributaries empty into the Dead Sea, but there are no outlets. Consequently, the hot sun evaporates the water, leaving a high mineral and salt content in which life cannot exist. When we do not have outlets of service, we become like the Dead Sea.

The Spirit-Filled Life

Where are you in the Spirit-filled life? Have you made a total surrender to Christ? Have you crucified the "self" so that Jesus has total reign in your life? Paul said: "I have been crucified with Christ; it is no longer I who live, but Christ lives in me; and the life which I now live in the flesh I live by faith in the Son of God, who loved me and gave Himself for me" (Galatians 2:20). The Holy Spirit wants to fill these earthen vessels. The Holy Spirit wants to get deep down inside of us and make us like Jesus. He wants to take us over and make us over. He wants to dwell and work inside us daily, controlling our thoughts and emotions, purifying our desires and motives and directing our wills and ambitions. The Holy Spirit is God's greatest gift, for God is actually offering Himself.

It is like the bridegroom who has given many gifts to his intended bride . . . perfume, candy, flowers, clothes, but at the altar of the church he comes and makes the final gift of himself. Without the giving of himself all the other gifts would be meaningless, but with the giving of himself they find fulfillment.

In the days of the Roman Empire lived a wealthy Roman senator who had only one son. The father made out his will, leaving everything to the boy, whom he loved dearly. But as the days went by, the son became more rebellious, disobedient and quarrelsome. Finally, he went into a rage, left home and was heard of no more. In desperation, the father rewrote his will, leaving everything he had to a trusted slave, with one provision: If the son returned home, he could choose only one thing out of the entire estate. On hearing of his father's death, the wayward son returned home only to learn of the change in the will. Everything now belonged to his father's slave. But he could choose one thing out of the whole estate. Should he choose a house in which to live or a field to cultivate? He pointed to the slave and said, "I'll take him." In choosing the slave he received the entire inheritance, for it was wrapped up in the person of the slave.

When we receive the fullness of the Holy Spirit by faith, we receive power, boldness, courage, stamina and love. God through His Son Jesus offers Himself in the Holy Spirit. He can give nothing higher. How can we settle for anything less?

My son, LenPaul, played a lot of "hide and go seek." He loved to hide from me behind the sofa. He even crawled under the dining table, or moved behind a chair. Though he loved to hide, his real joy came when I found him. If I acted as if I were not going to find him, he would rush out into my arms.

Now is the time to acknowledge where you are in your relationship to God. The truth may be painful, but God is ready to meet you where you are. God desires to pour out a fresh anointing of His Spirit on you and on His church. It requires only that we come out from behind the bush and confess our sin to Jesus Christ.

What on earth will you do for heaven's sake when you realize where you are in your relationship with Jesus Christ?

Chapter 13

It's Just a Matter of Trust

*I waited patiently for the L*ORD*; and He inclined to me, And heard my cry. He also brought me up out of a horrible pit,*
Out of the miry clay, and set my feet upon a rock, And established my steps. He has put a new song in my mouth—Praise to our God;
Many will see it and fear,
And will trust in the Lord. Blessed is the man who makes the Lord his trust,
And does not respect the proud nor such as turn aside to lies (Psalm 40:1–4).

But seek first the kingdom of God and His righteousness, and all these things shall be added to you. Therefore do not worry about tomorrow, for tomorrow will worry about its own things. Sufficient for the day is its own trouble (Matthew 6:33–34).

Here is a different twist to an age-old question: "What do you want to be when you grow up?" A child answered, "Taller."

Do we not desire to be taller in God's grace, more committed to Jesus and His church, more yielded to his blessed Holy Spirit? Do we not come seeking a deeper experience of God's grace? Then we need to stop worrying and start to trust God. Blessed is the person whose trust is in the Lord.

The basis of any personal relationship is trust. Trust forms the foundation of the marriage relationship. When that foundation is broken by an adulterous relationship, the marriage relationship suffers and may fail. Trust forms the foundation of parental relationships with children. Trust forms the foundation of our faith relationship with Jesus Christ.

Most people are worried about something right at this moment. Nearly everyone experiences some degree of anxiety and worry. I once asked my grandfather, a true saint in the Lord, what had robbed him most of his Christian joy. He promptly replied, "Son, it would be worry over things that never happened."

It is surprising how much energy we expend on things we can do nothing about. Here is how the anxiety of the average person is divided up:

40 percent—things that will never happen.
30 percent—things about the past that cannot be changed.
12 percent—criticism from others, mostly untrue.
10 percent—health, which gets worse with stress.
8 percent—real problems that will be faced.

Dr. Charles Mayo, of the Mayo Clinic, once said, "Half of all the beds in our hospitals are filled by people who worried themselves there." That is, worry and stress break down the immune system that subsequently makes the body more susceptible to diseases.

A huge crowd was watching the famous tightrope walker, Blondin, cross Niagara Falls one day in 1860. He crossed it

Chapter 13: It's Just a Matter of Trust

numerous times, a 1000-foot trip, 160 feet above the raging waters of Niagara Falls. The people called to him by name, "Blondin, Blondin, Blondin!" He turned to the crowd and said, "Do you believe in me?" And the crowd answered, "We believe, we believe, we believe." He announced to the crowd, "I'm going back across, and I'm going to take someone with me on my shoulders. Which one of you will it be?" Not a single word was spoken in that crowd of more than a thousand people.

Many of us are willing to shout, "We believe." But how many are willing to translate their belief into the kind of living that shows their belief?

The basic message of the Scripture is clear: Center your life upon God. Give Him first allegiance in your life and everything else will fall into place without worrying yourself sick over it. Jesus said, "Seek first the kingdom of God and His righteousness, and all these things shall be added to you. Therefore do not worry about tomorrow, for tomorrow will worry about its own things. Sufficient for the day is its own trouble."

The root word of "worry" means "to divide." When we worry about something, especially those things beyond our control, our allegiance is divided and we become unstable in our faith relationship. On the one hand, we trust God to work out everything. But on the other hand, we are in a dreadful state of anxiety.

Norman Vincent Peale tells about being stopped on the streets of New York by a man who said, "Reverend, I've got problems!" Dr. Peale answered, "Well, I know a place near here that has a population of fifteen thousand people and not one person has a single problem." His troubled friend said, "Tell me, where is this place? I'd like to live there." Dr. Peale answered, "It's Woodlawn Cemetery in the Bronx!"

To be alive is to have problems. We will not escape trials and tribulations in this life. To be a Christian does not exempt us from difficulties. Anybody who stands up to witness or preach and wears a pious grin on his face twenty-four hours a day is a phony. There are going to be dark days.

Some years ago one of the golfers on the pro tour was a pompous egomaniac. His emotional maturity was about that of a seven year old. He could do nothing wrong and always had a quick excuse for any loss.

As if these faults were not enough, he was also not above hustling a few extra dollars playing amateurs in cities on the tour for $50 a hole. One day a man wearing dark glasses and carrying a white cane offered to play him for $100 a hole.

"Why, I can't play you," the professional golfer protested. "You're blind, aren't you?"

"Yes, I am," replied the man. "But that's all right. I was a state champion before I went blind. I think I can beat you."

The conceited golfer had not been playing well lately, and he needed some extra money. Blind or not, if this guy was crazy enough to challenge him, why not? "You did say $100 a hole?" The blind man nodded. "Well, all right. It's a deal. But don't say I didn't warn you; you'll lose your money. When would you like to play?"

"Any night at all," replied the blind man, "any night at all."

Don't worry. God also works the night-shift. God may not always work in just the way we want Him to work. But can the God who clothes the lilies of the field and watches over the tiniest sparrow not be trusted with your life and mine? His eye is on the sparrow.

How do we stop worrying and start trusting? How can we start trusting God more? The formula is found in Psalm 40.

He Heard Me Cry

God hears the cry of His people. God hears the cry of anguish and calamity. You can place your trust in the God who hears your cry.

Chapter 13: It's Just a Matter of Trust

Jesus Christ trusted His heavenly Father. This is how Jesus could handle adversity and forgive His enemies. He trusted God even as He hung on the cross. Jesus knew that God heard His cry of anguish.

I recall my wife, Shana, getting up in the middle of a worship service and going to the church nursery. When the service was over, I asked why she had so abruptly left. "Was the sermon that bad?" I asked. She replied, "No, but I heard Shalen crying in the nursery so I went to get her." I could not believe she was able to distinguish the cry of our daughter from the cries of so many others. When I inquired about this, she simply said, "Lenny, don't you know that a mother knows the cry of her own child?" The same is true with God, for His heart toward us is more tender than a mother's heart.

An anonymous author has compiled a list called "Our Thinking vs. God's Promises."

We think: "It's impossible." God says, "All things are possible" (Matthew 19:26).

We think: "I'm too tired." God says, "I will give you rest" (Matthew 11:28).

We think: "Nobody really loves me." God says, "I love you" (John 3:16).

We think: "I can't go on." God says, "My grace is sufficient" (2 Corinthians 12:9).

We think: "I can't figure things out." God says, "I will direct your steps" (Proverbs 3:6).

We think: "I can't do it." God says, "You can do all things through Christ" (Philippians 4:13).

We think: "I can't forgive myself." God says, "I forgive you" (1 John 1:9).

We think: "I can't manage." God says, "I will supply all your needs" (Philippians 4:19).

We think: "I'm always worried and frustrated." God says, "Cast all your cares on Me" (1 Peter 5:7).

We think: "I feel so alone." God says, "I will never leave you nor forsake you" (Hebrews 13:5).

Based on these scriptural promises, we know that God hears our cry. Jesus trusted God and so can we!

He Lifted Me Up

Jesus said, "If I be lifted up, I will draw all people unto Me." The uplifting of Christ is God's gift to uplooking people. The miracle of miracles is that God gives us the grace to be "lifters" of His love. Not only does He lift us up, but also He gives us strength to lift up others. You can trust the God who lifts us up.

One of my favorite persons in the New Testament was from the island of Cyprus. He always brought laughter, hope and encouragement to people. He is not outspoken nor does he occupy a prominent place like Peter and Paul. His name was Barnabas—the encourager. Are you a Barnabas to someone?

If God lifts us through His grace and strength, then that must be the reason He gives us the Holy Spirit so that through His grace we can learn to be lifters and encouragers of one another.

The year was 1956. Dawson Trotman, founder of the Navigators, had taken a group of young people to a camp in upstate New York. He took a few children out in a boat and it capsized in the water. Dawson Trotman drowned while attempting to save those kids in that lake. The Reverend Billy Graham preached Dawson Trotman's funeral. Billy Graham said, "I think Dawson Trotman has touched more lives [for Christ] than anybody that I have ever known." In fact, the headlines in a national magazine read: "Dawson Trotman: Always Holding Somebody Up!"

Chapter 13: It's Just a Matter of Trust

Most of us do not become Christians because someone pulled us into the kingdom of God by a rope, nor are we Christians because someone had to twist our arm to accept Jesus Christ. Most of us become Christians because somebody made Jesus so real we could not turn him off. They kept flashing green lights in front of us: "You're loved! You're wanted! You're appreciated! This is the place for you!"

Can anyone say to you or to me, "Look, I'm going through the agony of a divorce, but it's because of your faith that I'm clinging to the Savior." "Look, I'm having a hard time. The doctor says it's terminal, but it's because of your love and prayers that I'm still being loyal to the fellowship." Can anybody say to you this day, "You're the reason why I'm pressing forward in the Christian faith?" If anybody can say that about us, we're wealthy—not by material standards but by God's standard.

He Gave Me a Song

I've been singing a new song ever since Jesus came into my life. It has not always been a constant song. There are days when it may not be sung in perfect pitch, but the lyrics are indelibly imprinted upon my mind and soul. You can trust the God who gives you a new song to sing.

Some of you know what it means to say with the prophet, "I've treaded the winepress alone." Some of you know what it's like to "walk through the valley of the shadow of death."

The glory is in returning to the Lord and being renewed in His strength. There come times when we need to be renewed in the faith. We stay alive in Jesus Christ as we are renewed and revived in our hearts by the Holy Spirit.

Somebody once said to Billy Sunday, "Revivals won't last." He said, "Neither does a bath, but it's a good thing to take every once in a while."

There was an old saint whose Bible was filled with notes written in the margin. Beside some of the verses the man had put the letters, "T. P." One day someone asked the old man what the letters meant. He responded, "Tried and proven."

God has sung a love song to the world. I happen to have the lyrics: "For God so loved the world that He gave His only begotten Son, that whoever believes in Him should not perish but have everlasting life." It makes life worth living, people worth loving and a message worth sharing.

A church bulletin printed this mistake in the title of the anthem: "Hallelujah, the Lord God Omnipotent Resigneth." Of course it was suppose to be, "Hallelujah, the Lord God Omnipotent Reigneth." God does reign and has not resigned! God is watching over us. Stop worrying and start trusting. Blessed is the person who makes the Lord his trust.

What on earth will you do for heaven's sake when you make the Lord your trust?

Chapter 14

Kamikaze Christians

Now it happened as they journeyed on the road, that someone said to Him, "Lord, I will follow You wherever You go."
And Jesus said to him, "Foxes have holes and birds of the air have nests, but the Son of Man has nowhere to lay His Head."
Then He said to another, "Follow Me."
But he said, "Lord, let me first go and bury my father."
Jesus said to him, "Let the dead bury their own dead, but you go and preach the kingdom of God."
And another also said, "Lord, I will follow You, but let me first go and bid them farewell who are at my house."
But Jesus said to him, "No one, having put his hand to the plow, and looking back, is fit for the kingdom of God" (Luke 9:57–62).

In an age when deficit financing is the norm rather than the exception, we have become for the most part people who do not worry about the "total cost." For that matter, we may not be much concerned about the monthly payments. "Get it now. Worry about paying for it later." This way of thinking has permeated our economic life.

Can it be that we look at our Christian commitment in the same way? We say we will follow Christ, but never intend to go all the way with Him to Jerusalem and Calvary. It is difficult to comprehend Dietrich Bonhoeffer's "Cost of Discipleship" and his pointed word, "the invitation to follow Christ is an invitation to come and die."

Church vows are certainly not made in this spirit. Support the church with your "attendance" is often interpreted to mean, "Come whenever it's convenient." Support the church with your "finances" is often understood to mean, "Remember the church with an offering, not a tithe, after you've paid the rent, cared for the monthly installments, or purchased something for yourself." Support the church with your "prayers" usually means no more than "tipping your hat to God" a few moments each day.

Jesus said, "If any man would come after me, let him deny himself and take up his cross and follow Me." When Jesus Christ confronts us and says, "Come and follow me," it is a radical demand being placed upon us.

The Breton fishermen live in the dangerous waters off the northwest coast of France. Often, storms and high winds and wave swells challenge them in the deep waters offshore as well as along rocky shores. Whenever they begin a trip that would require them to be weather-wise, they may be heard to pray: "Oh, God, Thy sea is so great and our boat is so small."

Christians today need to become aware of the gigantic task that is before the believing church. The sea of indifference, materialism, doubt, lust and greed is so great. Our world is so far from peace and the practice of a caring love in today's fragmented societies. Mighty forces of selfishness, racism, ignorance and fear come against our small boat. We are like the disciples in the boat that is sinking in the sudden storm that has struck the ship (Matthew 8:23–27). Our prayerful word must be, "Lord, save us! We are perishing."

American Christianity has been dangerously influenced by a growing secularization. The impact has led to a lessening of traditional forms of faith. It seems that too many of us are deciding that the Christian faith is relevant only to pockets of life rather than to the totality of living. Life in government, the market place, the classroom and sexuality is now a watered-down Judeo-Christian ethic. We have opted for freedom of choice and action with few limits.

Historically the roots of the Christian faith have centered in a passionate faith balanced between personal piety and a warm heart that cares about the hurt, selfishness, suffering and sin in an unsaved society. Yet too many of us succumb to a constant willingness to buy into current thought, to neglect personal morality and to emphasize a tolerant lifestyle that subtly says little is really absolutely essential in our faith walk. The church seems to be more human-centered at God's expense. We have lost our balance. We are no longer a holy people but people of the values of the world.

We live in a day of doubt. What we believe we do not believe very strongly. Often, what we disbelieve we tend to believe more strongly. The authority of the Bible is often questioned. Unfortunately, Jesus' cross of salvation has often been relegated to one among many ways to God. The uniqueness of Jesus Christ is found in His full deity and full humanity. The centrality of His ministry is discovered through His sacrifice on our behalf. Jesus Christ is the greatest and final revelation of God's mercy, love and grace.

The remedy for the ills of society lies in Jesus Christ. But His followers, true believers, are totally committed to

Christ and to His cause in the world. But what does it mean to be a follower of Jesus Christ?

During the Great Depression a pig and hen were walking by a church. On the board was a message: "These are hard times. Remember to feed the needy." The hen turned to the pig and said, "That's a great idea. I think we ought to get involved in that. Why don't you and I sponsor a ham and eggs breakfast?" The pig looked at the hen and said, "Friend, for you that's a contribution, but for me it's total commitment."

Jesus set up a "healing station" on the dusty road between Capernaum and Jerusalem. Eyes that rolled around in empty sockets searching the darkness within were now looking out on God's creation. Tongues that lay dormant for many years were now loosened and speaking forth praises to God. Limbs that once hung uselessly were now dancing and leaping. It was an exciting time as Jesus performed many miracles.

Jesus began interacting with three halfhearted followers—an impulsive one, a reluctant one, and a reserved one. Let's look at each of these interchanges.

The Impulsive Follower

First, there is the impulsive follower. This young man said to Jesus, "I will follow you wherever you go, Jesus." He wants to follow Jesus without counting the cost. His enthusiasm is dampened when Jesus tells him that he does not really know what he is doing.

Many of us have said the very same thing. Perhaps there was a time when you sensed the presence of God as never before. You became aware that Jesus was not merely a historical figure or legend but a living presence in your life. You heard the Spirit of God call and responded, "Jesus, I'll follow you." But look what Jesus said: "Foxes have holes, and birds of the air have nests; but the Son of man has no-

Chapter 14: Kamikaze Christians

where to lay His head." He shows the would-be disciple what life with Him entails.

Matthew 8, the parallel passage, tells us that this young man was a "scribe." He was a Jewish teacher of the Law. He was not ashamed to step aside from his peer group. This young man was ready to respond and quick with the spirit of volunteering.

A minister loves people like this young man. You don't have to get down on your knees and beg, or sing forty verses of "Just As I Am." John Wesley said, "Give me one hundred men who hate sin and fear God, and I will evangelize all of England!" If there were a hundred people with this type of willingness to serve, our community would be different.

But Jesus looks into this young man's heart and senses that he is impulsive. He is caught up in the excitement of the moment. Jesus looks at him and knows that nothing is wrong with the intention and his commitment, but the young man had not counted the cost of discipleship. Anytime you are totally committed to something it is going to cost you everything.

When Garibaldi set out to liberate Italy, he put together a ragtag army of volunteers. He called young men to follow him. One day someone in the crowd yelled: "Hey, Garibaldi, what are you going to give us for following you?" Garibaldi replied, "Hunger, torture, long marches, possibly death, but some of the most glorious victories of your life." He told them exactly what it would cost them, and Garibaldi went out to liberate Italy.

The resistance becomes most stubborn when you begin to break through the enemy's line. When you feel that the fighting is getting intense, you are most likely advancing in your Christian walk. You can always measure the weight of your blow against the enemy by the one you get back.

Is your Christianity costing you anything? If your Christianity is painless and costless, then it is most likely counterfeit.

The Reluctant Follower

Second, there is the reluctant follower. This young man was probably in the prime of life and standing in the midst of the crowd. Jesus wanted to challenge him so He looked into the eyes of the man's soul and said, "Follow Me." This would-be disciple wanted to bury his father before following.

An automobile factory in Detroit posted on their bulletin board the following: "The management regrets that it has come to their attention that workers are dying on the job and failing to fall down. This practice must stop, as it becomes impossible to distinguish between death and the natural movement of people. Any employee found dead in an upright position will be dropped from the payroll."

Many Christians are going through the motions. Some in the church are spiritually dead in an upright position— no life, no vitality, no zeal.

Look at what the young man said: "Lord, let me first go and bury my father." Now that is a reasonable request. But Jesus said, "Leave the dead to bury their own dead; but as for you, go and proclaim the kingdom of God."

A missionary in Turkey suggested that a wealthy young Turkish friend take a trip around the world. The young man said, "Well, I would like to but first I must bury my father." The missionary said, "I'm sorry. I did not realize that he had died." The Turk replied, "My father is not dead but is healthy. You see, it is our custom that we stay home with our parents until they are dead and then we bury them. Then, we are free to go." The whole process of staying with the family until the father dies is called "burying the father."

The young man was saying to Jesus, "You may have a claim on my life, but my family also has an important claim on my life. Something else has prior claim to your claim on my life."

Chapter 14: Kamikaze Christians

The Reserved Follower

Finally, there is the reserved follower. This young man said, "I will follow you, Lord; but let me first say farewell to those at my home." This would-be disciple is like the first. He thinks that following Jesus means that he must make the offer on his own initiative, as if it were a career he had mapped out for himself. He wants to dictate his own terms. But Jesus replied. "No one who puts his hand to the plow and looks back is fit for the kingdom of God."

Look at the man's request, "Lord, I want to go back and say farewell to my family." This man has one foot in his own kingdom and the other in Jesus' kingdom. He wanted only a part-time commitment!

Jesus encounters us and says, "Follow me. Lay down your life for me. Give up what you want for me." But we say, "Lord, I'm sorry. My children are only now starting school. I bought a new house. I have to wait until I retire."

Jesus Christ is looking for people who are totally committed to Him. Impulsive, reluctant, reserved followers quickly burn out.

In the last years of World War II, Japan began using kamikaze pilots, who volunteered to fly planes loaded with bombs directly into smokestacks of American ships. Of course the pilot perished with the plane. The Japanese called on 15-, 16-, and 17-year-old young men for this mission. They had more than enough volunteers. Why did they do it? It was for the glory of their country.

Jesus was looking for kamikaze-type followers, those who are willing to follow Him to the point of losing their lives.

Jesus Christ asks us, "Is your life and service to Me to be a contribution of a weekend here and there, or are you making a total commitment of your life?"

Jesus Christ is calling for His church to be filled with kamikaze Christians. Just think—what on earth you could do for heaven's sake if you become a kamikaze Christian?

Chapter 15

Resurrection Power

Mary stood outside by the tomb weeping, and as she wept she stooped down and looked into the tomb. And she saw two angels in white sitting, one at the head and the other at the feet, where the body of Jesus had lain. Then they said to her, "Woman, why are you weeping?"
She said to them, "Because they have taken away my Lord, and I do not know where they have laid Him."
Now when she had said this, she turned around and saw Jesus standing there, and did not know that it was Jesus. Jesus said to her, "Woman, why are you weeping? Whom are you seeking?"
She, supposing Him to be the gardener, said to Him, "Sir, if You have carried Him away, tell me where You have laid Him, and I will take Him away."
Jesus said to her, "Mary!"

> *She turned and said to Him, "Rabboni!" (which is to say, Teacher).*
> *Jesus said to her, "Do not cling to Me, for I have not yet ascended to My Father; but go to My brethren and say to them, I am ascending to My Father and your Father, and to My God and your God."*
> *Mary Magdalene came and told the disciples that she had seen the Lord, and that He had spoken these things to her (John 20:11–18).*

> *... that I may know Him and the power of His resurrection, and the fellowship of His sufferings, being conformed to His death, if, by any means, I may attain to the resurrection from the dead (Philippians 3:10–11).*

A group of four-year-olds was gathered in Sunday school class. The teacher looked at the class and asked, "Does anyone know what today is?" A little girl held up her hand and said, "Yes, today is Palm Sunday!" The teacher exclaimed, "That's wonderful! Now, does anyone know what next Sunday is?" Another little girl held up her hand and said, "Yes, next Sunday is Easter Sunday." Once again the teacher said, "That's fantastic! Now, does anyone know what makes next Sunday Easter?" Little Johnny was tired of the girls getting so much attention, so he held up his hand and said, "Yes, next Sunday is Easter because Jesus rose from the grave," and before the teacher could brag on him, he kept talking and said, "But if He sees His shadow, He has to go back in for six weeks."

The good news of Easter is that Jesus did not see His shadow and go back into the tomb. He is risen—just as He said!

A few years ago an eye-catching ad appeared in a Milwaukee, Wisconsin, newspaper's classified section. In large bold letters the headline of the ad read: "USED TOMB-

Chapter 15: Resurrection Power

STONE." Under the headline were these words: "Used tombstone for sale. Real bargain for someone. Signed, "Dingo."

I would love to know the rest of that story. Who in the world was this person named "Dingo," and why did he no longer need a tombstone?

The idea or image of a used tombstone may at first appear somber or depressing. But think about it again. A used tombstone means that its previous owner no longer has any use for it. It has become an unnecessary item.

This is precisely what the Easter story is all about. The message is clear: The tomb is empty. The grave marker is no longer needed. Jesus Christ has conquered death. Grammatically speaking, Good Friday was not a "period." It was not an "exclamation point." It was only a "comma" because God will always have the last word! God gave the victory, and Jesus Christ is alive.

The religious authorities wanted Jesus dead. It was a week of betrayal, arrest, denial and crucifixion. The disciples wanted Jesus alive but they knew He was dead. They had witnessed His crucifixion. They saw the Roman soldier pierce His side with a spear. They watched as His body was removed from the cross. They prepared it for burial and laid it in a borrowed tomb.

Then something happened on the third day. God raised Jesus Christ from the dead. The disciples thought He was dead. He *was* dead. But they discovered He was alive on that first Easter. The bodily resurrection of Jesus Christ empowered His disciples, and their faith came alive.

The message today is clear. The Lord is risen, and He shares the power of His resurrection with us. As Christians, we, too, have been resurrected. We, too, have new life. When we became Christians, we, too, made a new start. We, too, rose from tombs that imprisoned us!

The resurrection power of Jesus Christ also will help you rise above your problems, your pressure points and your heartaches. When trouble strikes, resurrection power will help you rise above it. When someone hurts you, resurrection power will help you rise above it. When you feel discouraged, resurrection power will help you rise above it.

Sometimes the Good Fridays we face threaten to do us in and bury us. But then along comes Easter to remind us that God ultimately wins. At Calvary evil had its best chance to defeat God but evil did not win.

Several years ago, *The Saturday Evening Post* ran a cartoon showing a man about to be rescued. He had been shipwrecked on a tiny deserted island and completely separated from civilization. The sailor in charge of the rescue team stepped onto the beach and handed the man a stack of newspapers. The sailor said, "With compliments from the Captain. But first he would like for you to glance at the headlines to see if you'd still like to be rescued!"

There are times when we feel that evil is winning and has the upper hand. But Easter reminds us that there is "no grave deep enough, no seal imposing enough, no stone heavy enough, no evil strong enough to keep Jesus in the grave."

The resurrection of Jesus Christ empowers the Christian to face not only the fear of dying but also the challenge of living. It gives us a lasting foundation on which to build our lives.

This is the reality of Easter, and it can be ours today. That is why the Apostle Paul said, "That I may know Him and the power of His resurrection." Jesus was resurrected, and on that first Easter the disciples also rose from their spiritual and emotional graves. Here are three examples.

Rise above Despair

First, through the power of Christ's resurrection you can rise above despair. In John's Gospel, Mary Magdalene is a dramatic symbol of victory over despair (John 20:11–18). On that first Easter morning, she came to the tomb

Chapter 15: Resurrection Power

weeping, filled with despair and sadness. She had lost someone she loved. She was brokenhearted. Someone close to her had died, and she was devastated.

Several years before the Gulf War, a reporter did a story on gender roles in Kuwait. She noted then that women customarily walked about ten feet behind their husbands. This same reporter recently returned to Kuwait and observed that the men now walked several yards behind their wives. She approached a Kuwaiti woman and asked, "This is marvelous! Can you tell the free world just what enabled women here to achieve this reversal of roles?" The woman quickly replied, "Land mines."

Figuratively speaking, Mary Magdalene could have been walking into a minefield as she made her way toward the tomb on that first Easter morning. The Jews were cautious and fearful. They certainly did not want any rumors to surface about a resurrection. They had guarded the tomb with Roman soldiers.

No experience in human life is more universal than sorrow and grief. Most of us have lost loved ones. Most of us know that terrible feeling. George Bernard Shaw once said, "Life's ultimate statistic is the same for all; one out of one dies."

A painful fact of life is that the reality of death comes to each one of us. Someone we love has died or will die one day. That fact alone can fill us with despair. Like a heavy blanket, despair covers us and smothers the very life out of us. It may be like a tomb and imprison us. It may choke our vitality and zest for living. That's what Mary felt as she hurried to the tomb on that first Easter morning. She felt despair.

She came looking for a dead body, but she found the risen Lord. When she encountered the risen Jesus she, too, rose to new hope. No more sorrow. No more despair. No more weeping. Suddenly, she burst out of her tomb of despair and ran back to the disciples, shouting, "I have seen the Lord! I have seen the Lord! He is risen!"

One of the most beloved sports personalities of our time was Jim Valvano. Across the sports world he was known affectionately as "Jimmy V." After a yearlong battle with cancer, Jim Valvano died in 1993 at the age of 47. He is remembered as the great basketball coach who took the North Carolina State Wolfpack to the 1983 National Championship in Houston, Texas.

Most of all, Jim Valvano will be remembered for his courage, for the courageous way he faced and rose above a horrible, debilitating illness. A few weeks before he died he was honored on national television at a major basketball game. He stood before thousands and a television audience as he said, "My friends, today I fight a different battle. You see, I have trouble walking, and I have trouble standing for a long period of time. The cancer is attacking and destroying my body. But what cancer cannot touch are my mind, my heart and my soul. I have faith in God and hope that things might get better for me. But if they don't, I promise you this—I will never, ever give up."

His 1983 championship team was present. He then pointed to them and said, "I learned a great lesson from these guys. They amazed me. They did things I never dreamed they could do because they absolutely refused to give up. That's the lesson I learned from them. Don't ever, ever give up! And that's the message I leave with you. Never give up!"

Even though we may feel like giving up when someone we love dies, the resurrection power of Christ enables us to rise above despair. God wins over death, and He wants to share His victory with us.

Rise above Disillusionment

Second, through the power of Christ's resurrection you can rise above disillusionment. In Luke's Gospel (24:13–35), Cleopas and his companion are dramatic symbols of victory over disillusionment as they walked to Emmaus.

Chapter 15: Resurrection Power

When people try something and it doesn't live up to their expectations, they are disillusioned. They feel let down. They turn away with disappointment. They may even feel a sense of betrayal and bitterness.

A young couple was on a fast track in their social life. They were ambitious and wanted to climb the social ladder. Hoping to make an impression on the wealthy and elite in their community, they went to the social matriarch of their city, who was a friend. They not only asked for her advice but also asked her to lend a priceless necklace of natural pearls for a special dinner meeting. After some thought, the wealthy lady consented and lent the pearls to the young lady. Unfortunately, the pearls were stolen that same night. In a panic, the couple went to a distant emporium. They described the necklace to a master jeweler and had the strand recreated. The cost was so enormous that it would take them years to repay. Suddenly, their ambition for fame, fortune and social prominence was gone with the pearls. The new pearls would cost them everything they had. They took the replacement necklace to the wealthy woman.

Several years later, the wealthy lady was about to die. Out of guilt and respect the young woman went to her bedside and confessed the whole charade. The older woman rose from her bed and said: "Those were fake pearls. No one ever lends the real ones. You've wasted your life on fake pearls!"

Be careful that you do not go through life and come to the end only to realize you have worked, learned, loved and played for fake pearls.

That's the picture we see in Cleopas and his companion as they walked toward Emmaus. Disappointment, disillusionment, heartbrokenness and hopelessness characterized their steps. They knew about the crucifixion, but they had not yet encountered the risen Lord. Their conversation might have gone something like this: "We thought He was the one to save us. We should have known better. It was too good to be true. And now it's over."

This is a portrait of disillusionment. But look what happens. The risen Lord comes to them. He walks with them. He talks to them. The power of His resurrection helps them to rise above their disillusionment. They come out of the tomb of disillusionment and rush back to the other disciples.

We will still have dark moments, but like Mary Magdalene and Cleopas and millions of others since, the resurrection of Jesus Christ will help you rise above the disillusionments and disappointments in life.

Rise above Defeat

Finally, through the power of Christ's resurrection you can rise above defeat. In the Easter story, Simon Peter is a dramatic symbol of victory over defeat (John 21:15-19). Peter had been so brash, so confident, so cocky. But when crunch-time came, he failed miserably. He had denied his Lord three times. He had been defeated. But the risen Lord came to Peter at the Sea of Galilee. Resurrection power was giving him another chance.

Jesus asked Peter three times, "Simon, do you love me? Then feed my sheep." The risen Lord was saying, "Peter, you have a job to do. You are not defeated. You can bounce back. You fell down, but you can get up. Don't quit on me, now, Peter. Rise above this defeat."

Paderewski was Poland's most famous pianist. He was also the prime minister of Poland. During his long and illustrious career, Paderewski scheduled a concert in a small village. It was his hope to cultivate the arts in rural Poland. A young mother, wishing to encourage her son's interest in the piano, bought tickets for the Paderewski performance.

When the night of the concert arrived, they found their seats near the front of the music hall. A beautiful grand piano stood on the stage. The mother went over and visited with some friends before the concert. Quietly, the little boy slipped out of his mother's sight. When eight o'clock arrived,

Chapter 15: Resurrection Power

the spotlight came up on center stage. The audience noticed the ten-year-old boy seated at the grand piano, innocently picking out "Twinkle, Twinkle, Little Star."

His mother could not believe her eyes. The stagehands stepped out to grab the boy, but suddenly Paderewski appeared on the opposite side and waved them away. The master musician quickly moved to the piano and stood behind the little boy. He then whispered into his ear, "Don't quit. Keep on playing!" Leaning over, Paderewski reached down with his left hand and began to fill in some bass notes. Then his right arm reached around the other side of the boy. Now encircling the boy, the master and the young novice held the crowd mesmerized with great music. It was a wonderful moment.

Nothing transforms life more than when the Master, Jesus Christ, surrounds us with His arms of love and whispers in our hearts time and again, "Don't quit on life. Keep on living. For I am the resurrection and life; he who believes in me, though he die, yet shall he live" (John 11:25).

Christians are people who proclaim the empty tomb. You can receive new life in Jesus Christ today. You can have a new chance, a new start, a new life. You can experience the resurrection power of Jesus. You can rise above your despair. You can rise above your disillusionment. You can rise above your defeat.

What on earth will you do for heaven's sake with God's resurrection power?